LOVING
LAGUNA

A LOCAL'S GUIDE TO
LAGUNA BEACH

UPDATED + REVISED

SKIP HELLEWELL

To Frank and Sue Tanner
who back in 1958 brought a group of
Boy Scouts from Sacramento to
Laguna Beach with the promise of
teaching them how to surf.

CONTENTS

The Roots of Laguna's Uniqueness

This book is a guide for the thoughtful person—resident or visitor—who wishes to wiggle their feet deep into the sand and understand what makes Laguna Beach so unique. But it's more than a travel guide, as you'll see. The roots of Laguna's uniqueness are varied, some physical, others more ethereal.

The coastal range that physically separates Laguna from inland regions, over eons of wearing by waves, formed the coves that make Laguna's beaches unique. It's likely those same hills that kept Laguna from being a land grant ranch in the Spanish and Mexican eras, thus saving a place for the homesteading families of the 1870s. Those homesteaders were people of faith: their first collective effort was to form a church.

That coastal range forms our marine layer, the seasonal fog bank that's our natural air conditioner. Folks from Riverside came in the beginning to escape the summer heat. They brought their faith with them and funded a town hall for Sunday meetings. Next came the artists, beginning with Norman St. Clair, drawn here by the beauty of those coves. They were *plein air* painters, and in the work of these early California impressionists, one can see a deep reverence for Nature. The survival of the art colony was ensured when that town hall was converted into a gallery to sell their paintings.

Later the wave riders discovered Laguna. If you visit with a surfer, you'll find a reverence for nature akin to the early artists. The ocean moves them in many ways. Hawaiian surfers brought the aloha spirit— a way of bonding with family, community, and Nature—that distinguishes the true waterman.

So the roots of Laguna's uniqueness run deep. It's a premise of this book that having understood Laguna, you're a step closer to understanding what makes you, the reader, unique. And that, I think, makes this much more than a travel guide.

 = Editor's pick

AT LEFT: The Agrarian Age meets the Industrial Age in this nostalgic (c. 1912) Forest Avenue photo—horses and automobiles equably share the unpaved street. The Isch Warling Palace Livery, a bed and breakfast for horses, stood behind the cameraman. But down Forest a banner for Roy Peacock's new garage offers services for autos.

Other businesses were getting started, though the *café* on the left and *bakery* on the right have only generic names, as if there were no competitors. Fred Clapp, on the other hand, has added his name to the top of the sign for the General Store. Look down the street and you can see the sign for Laguna Cliffs. This was Howard Heisler's north Laguna subdivision—advertised as the tract with water. The sign didn't bother to mention the gorgeous ocean views. In early Laguna, just about everyone had an ocean view, but piped water was a luxury.

All the picture lacks is a *plein air* artist working at his easel, but artists likely made the store signs. Out of sight at the end of the road an enterprising young man named Joe Jahraus has opened a needed business—a lumberyard. Soon, 1915 to be exact, the county will pave a single-lane road down Laguna Canyon and this sleepy town by the sea will start to bustle. In time everyone will have water and ocean views will become a luxury. And just like today, you'll feel fortunate to find a parking space on Forest Avenue. *Credit: Photo from First American, courtesy of the Laguna Beach Historical Society.*

WALKING THROUGH HISTORY

To understand the roots of Laguna's uniqueness you have to get your feet on the ground. Here are five walks, plus a stroll through the historic Hotel Laguna. If your time is limited on this trip, visit Heisler Park in the freshness of the morning, and then stroll up Forest Avenue after brunch. Truth be told, the walks are great any time of day, especially at sunset.   *Photo: David Laws*

In the beginning everyone in the scattered settlements—Laguna Canyon, Laguna Beach, Arch Beach, and along Aliso Creek—was some kind of farmer. The family farm was the founding institution of early America. Search your family tree and you'll find farmers within a few generations. We remember those early settlers in Section VII.

In the second Laguna Beach period two new professions emerged: artist and merchant. (We'll talk about the artists in Section III.) Those first merchants learned that making a business was different from farming; the early Laguna farmers struggled when they tried their hand at business. The critical parameters were different: capital, for example, replaced land as the resource to be protected. Though the farmers settled the area, it was the business people who shaped the town, as you'll see in our walk through history.

CHAPTER 1
Heisler Park

Getting started: To start this walk (by car) drive up Coast Hwy 0.7 mile from Main Beach and turn left at Cliff Drive. (Beverly goes to the right; to the left the street is Cliff Drive. Cliff Dr. touches Coast Hwy in three places and you want the middle place.) Once on Cliff Dr. look for a place to park. (Parking is free on the streets above Heisler Park; meters adjacent to the park are $2/Hr. and take quarters or credit cards.) Allow 1-2 hours for this walk, depending on what catches your interest; a jogger could do it in 15 minutes.

DIRECTIONS This is a loop walk. Take the path along the bluff first and return via the Cliff Drive sidewalk. At the mid-point (Las Brisas Restaurant) continue on Cliff Drive to Coast Highway to admire the scene before returning.

SIGHTS OF INTEREST

There are stairs from the main walkway down to the coves below Heisler Park. The beaches, starting from the north end:

Fisherman's Cove, the beach below Boat Canyon, is a protected bay that paddle boarders like because of the gentle surf. But there is the task of carrying paddleboards down and back up the stairs. For paddleboard resources see Chapter 18.

Diver's Cove (as well as Shaw's Cove, ¼ mile north) is a favorite with divers because of the reefs and kelp beds that harbor fish. Southern

The Victor Hugo Inn opened in 1938, featuring fine food and beautiful grounds as shown in this view looking towards Main Beach. *Photo: Tom Pulley Postcard Collection, courtesy of the Laguna Beach Historical Society.*

California's best diving spots are found in Laguna Beach. For diving information, see Chapter 18.

Picnic Cove actually is a good place for a picnic, whether on the beach or in the grassy area above.

Public Art is found all over Laguna. Look to the left for the steel sculpture titled "Breaching Whale." You'll see more on your walk.

Rock Pile Beach is a longish narrow beach with rocky areas but also sandy nooks where you can be alone. This is one of three designated surfing beaches so is off-limits to swimmers. (The other surfing areas are named for nearby streets: St. Ann's, Brooks, and Thalia, plus Agate at certain times.)

Bird Rock is a designated bird refuge so can't be visited. In 1896 the townspeople and James Irvine, who put up the land and $100, built a wharf out to Bird Rock. For posts they used eucalyptus trees cut from the canyon. The pier was built to attract visitors and facilitate fishing around the kelp beds. It was improved in 1926 but disappeared in a series of storms in 1939.

Las Brisas offers a buffet breakfast with omelets to order. (Try the bread pudding.) Besides the food, there's a great view, making this a place to enjoy sunsets. Old-timers knew this as Victor Hugo's Inn (founded in 1938). Look for the landscape artist working nearby—he's a true Laguna character.

For movie buffs, the famous Bette Davis two-cigarette scene was shot on the patio of Las Brisas, known then as Victor Hugo's Inn, for the movie Now, Voyager. The movie also had the remembered line, "Let's not ask for the moon. We have the stars." At the time Davis was living in Laguna Beach so, really, besides the stars she had the beach. It was in another setting that she popularized the phrase, "What a dump."

DIRECTIONS Take the sidewalk past Las Brisas to the intersection at Coast Hwy, to see these sites (in clockwise order):

💜 **Laguna Art Museum** (SW corner; read more in Chapter 13) was the first dedicated art museum in Southern California and houses work of early Laguna painters. The museum, one of Laguna's best-kept secrets, is definitely worth visiting.

💜 **Indian Territory** (NW corner.) is a "must see" if you have an interest in indigenous art (basketry, pottery, jewelry, blankets). I don't think you'll find a better offering of antique Indian material this side of Santa Fe, New Mexico. Ask for a brief tour and you'll get an education in the rich art history of American Indians.

Urth Caffé (NE corner) offers organic heirloom coffee, tea, plus a breakfast and lunch menu. Once the home of Joe Skidmore, early businessman and stepson of Laguna founder Nate Brooks, after 1964 it was the Cottage restaurant. The Skidmore's picturesque 1917 craftsman cottage with Japanese influences was appropriately named sans souci, meaning "no worries."

This pier, built by townspeople in 1896 with help from James Irvine, was a community project long before there was an incorporated town. *Photo: First American, courtesy of the Laguna Beach Historical Society.*

Jahraus Park (the triangular park on SE corner) is a memorial to Elmer Jahraus, a founder of Laguna Beach; his son Joe founded Laguna Lumber. The statue Boy and Dog, by Ruth Peabody, 1933, is Laguna's oldest public art.

DIRECTIONS Return to your car via the Cliff Dr. sidewalk, observing:

Lawn Bowling was popular with well-behaved people in the '30s and we're still playing in Laguna. The Laguna Beach Lawn Bowling rinks were built in 1931. (For introductory lessons call 949/494 1811.)

Oldest Cliff Dr. home can be seen at 550 Cliff Dr. Built about 1907 as a board and batten cottage, it has been remodeled but still serves as a reminder of times past. This is the 7th oldest home in Laguna Beach.

PRAISE FOR MR. HEISLER

On your walk did you wonder who Heisler was? In 1905 Howard G. Heisler and his partners purchased north Laguna—the coastal ranch land from Laguna Creek (Broadway St. today) up to Emerald Bay—from the Irvine Ranch. Heisler and his partners named their tract Laguna Cliffs and reserved ½ mile of coastline for today's Heisler Park. He also helped the Laguna Beach Art Association obtain land for today's Laguna Art Museum, encouraged Pomona College to build their Marine Laboratory here in 1913 (see Chapter 5), and built the Heisler Building on Coast Highway.

A photo taken c. 1912 (see page 6) shows a real estate office on Forest Avenue with Laguna Cliff's main claim: "The tract with water." In those days, water was scarce so Heisler ran a pipe down from a well in the canyon. The lots along Cliff Drive enjoy wonderful views but were slow to sell—it was a long trip to Laguna by horse and buggy. But Heisler was prescient—the automobile age was coming—and Cliff Dr. soon became a prestigious address. In recent years the city allowed condominium projects to be built on those lots and the street lost some of its luster, but the park endures as a marvelous gift.

CHAPTER 2

Main Beach, Laguna's Window-to-the-Sea

The lifeguard tower is a Laguna icon. It's the most-photographed, sketched, and painted building in town, maybe on the Pacific coast. Originally the office for a gas station across Coast Hwy, it has served our lifeguards since 1937. How many pretty girls have walked by and smiled at a lifeguard? Thousands, I suppose. *Photo: April H. Dickson*

DIRECTIONS: There are no directions and no certain time for this walk. But to better appreciate our town, spend an hour or so checking out the Main Beach denizens. There's much to do here: you can sit in the sun, enjoy the beach or the playground, take a walk, play volleyball or basketball, and even chess.

Main Beach is a beach to be sure, but it's also a three-ring circus. Just sit down on one of the benches and observe. Where can you find a more entertaining scene? The grassy area by the Isch Building is home to the protesting class—over the years about just everything has been the target of someone's protest.

The icons are aligned in this Main Beach study: the boardwalk, lifeguard building, American flag, and Hotel Laguna bell tower. *Photo: David Laws*

Take a walk:

Walk south along the waterline; this is Laguna's longest stretch of beach not interrupted by coves so you can go as far as your legs will carry you. The bluff lots south of the Hotel Laguna were the first to be offered for sale, beginning in 1883, and sold quickly to Riverside folks who were doing well thanks to a new crop: oranges.

The Riverside people and their cottages are gone now but they left a gift important to Laguna's development as an art colony: They donated $100, a sizable sum then, towards a community center. The townspeople built a hall in the parking lot of today's Hotel Laguna. Known as the "Pavilion," it had a raised stage at one end. The building was used for town meetings, Sunday school, dances, socials, plays, weddings, and funerals. In 1918 it became Laguna's first art gallery and the success of that show led to an artist association and all that followed. When the new Art Gallery opened in 1928, the Laguna Beach Hotel was to be razed, so the old Pavilion needed a new home. Fred Swankowsky, concert pianist and artist, moved the building to 571 Graceland and made it his home. It remains a residence to this day, expanded and restored.

You can see the remains of homes built too close to the water and lost in the El Nino storms of the '90s. The most interesting remaining home on the bluff above the beach features a shingled turret with a wide veranda. You'll recognize it, about a block south of the Hotel Laguna. Thomas Harper, a noted early Laguna architect, designed this eclectic 1928 residence for a successful inventor. The address is 629 S. Coast but it's most visible from the beach. (Sources include *Cottages and Castles*, Karen Nelson Turnbull, 1987)

How We Got Main Beach Back

Back in the 1880s, when folks from Santa Ana and Riverside started spending summers at Laguna, they provided jobs for the locals who otherwise might have starved. After a single-lane highway for automobiles was paved down Laguna Canyon in 1915 the crowds got bigger, especially on the 4th of July.

As the years passed, hotels, restaurants, art galleries, and tourist shops sprung up along the coastline, blocking the ocean views that made Laguna famous. The long-gone Cabrillo Ballroom, offering "clean dancing every night but Sunday," was a destination during the Big Band Era. Hollywood stars, including Judy Garland and Mickey Rooney, danced here it's said. When the Big Bands died after WWII, the ballroom became a bowling alley.

The problem was that when you came down the canyon into town, you couldn't see the ocean for all the buildings. So from the beginning there was a desire to restore main beach—to open a "window to the sea." The campaign to do this lasted decades; election were held to approve bonds and though most were in favor the necessary two-thirds majority proved elusive.

During this time the Festival of Arts had grown in importance. The Festival of Arts venue is rented from the city and in 1968 they offered to accept a rent increase sufficient to finance a bond to buy Main Beach back. It was a remarkable offer and a big-hearted payback to the city that created them. In 1968 the city acquired the beach properties (its largest financial transaction) and the new Main Beach was dedicated in 1974. Cities don't normally buy land just to return it to Nature but this set a precedent for an even bigger project—the Laguna Greenbelt, a story told in Chapter 33. *(Source: April 1998 lecture by Vern Spitaleri at L.B. Historical Society.)*

CHAPTER 3

The Hotel Laguna

Hotel, Laguna Beach, Cal.

The Laguna Beach Hotel: Back in the 1880s Henry and Hub Goff, enterprising brothers, each built a hotel. Hub Goff built the Arch Beach Hotel down on Diamond Street in 1886, and it got off to a good start. Near this site his brother Henry built and later sold what became the Laguna Beach Hotel. The new owner, desiring an ocean view, moved the structure to this site. Unfortunately, the real estate boom of the 1880s was followed by a crash in the early 1890s and both hotels closed.

Joseph Yoch, a Santa Ana businessman with good timing, purchased and revived the Laguna Beach Hotel. Foreseeing more demand, he bought the defunct Arch Beach Hotel, moved it to Laguna in sections, and expanded the Laguna Beach Hotel to 30 rooms (with all of two baths)—the building in this picture. The Laguna Beach Hotel became the town's leading hotel and gathering place and remained in operation until 1928 when it was razed. *Photo: Courtesy Orange County Archives.*

GETTING STARTED: This walk (just 200 ft. long) starts at the front door of the Hotel Laguna. Start around noon and if you're hungry enjoy a meal on the ocean view terrace (there's also indoor dining for those rare cold days). Pause a moment in the hallway to check out the old pictures of Laguna scenes or the original register open to 1931. The time for this walk could be 10 minutes or two hours, depending on your curiosity and hunger.

The Hotel Laguna: The 70-room Hotel Laguna, built in Mission revival style with faux bell tower, was constructed in just 60 days in 1930 to replace the Laguna Beach Hotel. The tower was originally crowned with a "Hotel Laguna" sign, a sort of lighthouse for weary travelers, but a sign ordinance forced its removal in 1966. The hotel was easily the grandest building in Laguna and has served the town well for over 80 years.

It was hard times for the hotel business during the Depression but movies were coming out with "sound"—so up in Hollywood business was booming. The Hotel Laguna hitched its wagon to this new technology, touting the benefits of making movies in charming Laguna with beach, hills, and countryside for outdoor scenes. As movies were filmed here, Hollywood stars began to visit and buy beach homes. The old hotel register would be a great source for a Laguna history project. Notable guests include Hollywood stars such as Humphrey Bogart, Errol Flynn, and John Barrymore, who may have appreciated it as a romantic hideaway. The Hotel Laguna is a Laguna Beach landmark and has been for over 80 years. The bell tower, like the lifeguard tower on Main Beach, is a much photographed and painted Laguna icon. To really know this town, you have to know the Hotel Laguna.

The Hotel Laguna: This c. 1940 postcard shows the Hotel Laguna with the original roof sign—a light house of sorts for weary travelers. In the '30s the hotel bustled with Hollywood film crews and actors shooting movies with "sound." In WWII it served as an officers barrack. Over the years it was a popular romantic getaway. If the walls could talk— the stories they'd tell. *Photo: Tom Pulley Postcard Collection, courtesy of Laguna Beach Historical Society.*

CHAPTER 4

Forest Avenue Historic Shopping District

"The Gate" was the name of the first ice cream shop, opened by Carl Hofer in 1915 after the town got electricity. This hanging gate with verse, it's said, is original. *Photo: April Hellewell Dickson.*

TIME: Allow ½ -2 hours depending on your curiosity and shopping instincts; distance is about 1 mile in a loop that returns to the starting point. Keep your eye open for an art gallery that fits your interest.

DIRECTIONS: Start where Forest and Park intersect at Coast Highway, under the hanging gate. Walk up Forest on the right side to Second St. Return 100 ft. to the crosswalk at Beach St. and cross to the other side and continue up Forest to the corner (3rd St ends at the stop sign). Pause (see notes) then take the crosswalk and continue up Forest to the crosswalk at Ocean St. Take Ocean to Beach, pause at the corner (see notes), then turn left on Beach, right on Forest, and return to your starting point.

202 Park (Chantilly Ice Cream) Carl Hofer opened a Laguna ice cream parlor in 1915, the year they paved a single-lane road down Laguna Canyon and the town got electricity. He held a contest to name the business and the best idea came from an English pub called The Gate. When Hofer moved to this site he brought the gate along (look up).

241, 245, 255 Forest: The 1926 arrival of Coast Highway ignited a building boom on Forest Avenue. These 1928 brick buildings had shops below and offices above. They still do.

Fred Aufdenkamp built #255. The Aufdenkamp family owned Laguna's movie theatres: the Lynn (for silent movies), then the New Lynn (now the Laguna South Coast, built for sound movies). Fred and his brother built log cabin homes behind this store (where the Laguna Beach Library stands now).

💜 **295 Forest:** Roy Peacock came to Laguna around 1912 and opened an automotive garage on Forest. He later brokered insurance and real estate, and built this triangular building in 1926. Today it's the popular home accessories boutique, Tuvalu.

305 Forest: This Normandy Revival building with flanking turrets has been a landmark building on Forest since 1927. Designed in the Normandy Revival style by French-born architect Jean Egasse, and built by Elmer Jahraus (whose son commissioned the other Egasse building on Forest) the building housed the South Coast News for many years, then Eschbach's Florist.

💜 **361 Forest:** Check out Centrál, a hot new restaurant featuring coastal Peruvian dishes.

381 Forest: Check the information desk at *Visit Laguna Beach*, visit their website *visitlagunabeach.com* for "100 Things to Do", or ask about the app for tracking Laguna's free trolleys.

415 Forest: The Laguna Presbyterian Church is an uplifting presence on Forest Avenue. The original sanctuary dates to 1928 (Laguna bustled with construction that year) and the style is Gothic inspired Mediterranean Revival. For more see Chapter 31.

DIRECTION: Retrace your steps to the Beach St. crosswalk, cross over and continue up Forest to the intersection with 3rd St.

439 Forest: It's across the street, but admire the charming brick building of Live Wire Cleaners. Clothing has been cleaned here since the 1920s.

384 Forest: (the street numbers on the two sides of Forest are offset) Joe Jahraus founded the Laguna Beach Lumber Company on this corner in 1912. Laguna's source of lumber, until a single-lane road was paved through Laguna Canyon in 1915, had been driftwood, shipwrecks, and wood arduously carried by mules. Joe owned the first truck in Laguna and hauled lumber from the Irvine Santa Fe depot.

If you chose the building most important to Laguna's history this would be one of the finalists. Built in 1919, it was the home of Laguna Lumber until it moved to the canyon in 1975. The building then became a place to eat; for many years it was the Ivy House (ivy had grown to cover the roof); now it's simply the Lumberyard. *Photo: Skip Hellewell*

Jahraus served in France with the American Expeditionary Force during WWI and was drawn to the French Normandy architecture. On his return he commissioned Jean Egasse, a gifted architect of French origin, to design a building for his lumberyard. Joe, pleased with the result, imagined other buildings along the street in this style. Sadly, his father Elmer did the only other building (see 305 Forest, above).

Cross Forest Ave via the crosswalk at intersection with Third St.

306 Third St: This is the first in a row of Mediterranean Revival buildings designed by Aubrey St. Clair, son of the first artist to paint in Laguna. The Laguna Beach County Water District, founded by four Laguna citizens in 1926 when the well in the canyon turned sour, was the key to Laguna's growth. Nothing could happen without water. (Step inside to see a history display.)

501 Forest: The fire station was St. Clair's next public project, built in 1929. Take note of the sidewalk artwork titled *The People's Council*. The figures represent Man, Woman, and Youth; as the sun moves the shadow of the obelisk denotes guiding words.

505 Forest: The City Hall was built on the site of the "Old Ranch House" in 1951. The last owner was the Woman's Club; before leaving they extracted a promise to save the pepper tree (planted in the 1880s, it's said, by the Rogers family). The parking lot adjacent to City Hall becomes a lively Farmers' Market on Saturday mornings.

This has been Laguna's main fire station since 1929. The architect was Aubrey St. Clair, son of the artist who discovered Laguna and introduced it to other noted painters. *Credit: Laguna Beach Historical Society.*

Point of interest: At the end of Forest, Broadway turns into Laguna Canyon Rd. Though not part of this walk, note the cultural collection there: the Moulton Playhouse (Laguna's repertory theatre; 606 Laguna Canyon), the grounds for the Festival of Arts and the Pageant of the Masters' Irvine Bowl amphitheatre (650 Laguna Canyon). For more about these institutions, see Chapter 14. The "lighthouse" on the opposing hill was a creative way to vent fumes from Laguna's original sewage plant.

DIRECTIONS: Continue to the crosswalk, cross over to Ocean Ave.

Peter Blake Gallery, 435 Ocean, introduced contemporary art to Laguna Beach, an art colony built on traditional and Impressionist art, back in1993.

Corner of Ocean and Beach:

Pause to appreciate the neighborhood. Rasta Taco, a new shop on the NE corner, offers take-out. Whole Foods, on the NW corner, has healthy food and a deli, good for picnics. Down Ocean is the Laguna Beach Historical Society's cottage at #278 (open for tours and questions, Fri-Sun, 1:00 to 4:00). Further down at #207 is Areo, a great eco-friendly gift shop.   Just around the corner at 214 Beach is Wally's Barber Shop here since 1946. Wally is gone now but Rudy Campos is in his 6th decade of dispensing news along with haircuts.

This Forest Avenue picture was taken after 1916 (note the electric poles) and before 1926 (when Coast Hwy., in the foreground, was paved). You can see the "gate" at the drug store and soda fountain (on the right) that still marks the corner. Parking was free then; the parking meter wouldn't be invented until 1935. *Credit: First American, courtesy of Laguna Beach Historical Society.*

DIRECTIONS: Take a left on Beach St. and then right on Forest.

294 Forest: The Hobie Surf Shop is more than a store—it's the culmination of the beach culture that still defines coolness for American boys. For more on Hobie Alter see Chapter 19. The building, of Classical Revival design, was built in 1940.

Before leaving Beach Street note the 40-ft. bronze sculptural mural called Waterman's Wall, part of the Hobie Surf Shop. Hobie offers everything cool in surfing, housed in a 1940 Greek Revival building. For more on the late Hobie Alter, see Chapter 19.

280, 282 Forest: Built in 1917, this is one of the oldest commercial downtown buildings (the front has been remodeled). It was the first location of the old Excelsior Creamery, later at 302 Forest.

244 Forest: Bushard's Pharmacy, a Laguna family business since 1946, now entering its third generation.

234 Forest: A bakery since 1928, first Covern's, then Renaissance, finally Trotter's Bakery. It's Cucina Alessa today.

230 Forest: A produce market since the Brown family built it in 1923 with accordion doors that open to display fruit and vegetables. Since 1994 it's the 230 Forest Avenue restaurant.

CHAPTER 5

A Walk Down Coast Highway

The Pomona College Marine Laboratory, built in 1913 to teach ocean zoology, was Laguna's most impressive early building. *Credit: Photo by Beckquist, from the Ramsey Collection, courtesy of the Laguna Beach Historical Society.*

GETTING STARTED: Begin at the Main Beach Lifeguard Tower and walk south along Coast Highway five blocks to Cleo St. Cross over at the Cleo crosswalk and return. The first point of interest—the Pomona College Marine Laboratory—no longer exists but was across the street from the lifeguard tower, by Starbucks.

TIME: You could cover the ten blocks in a half-hour but a curious person might take 1-2 hours to see and appreciate. If it helps, there's food along the way.

Pomona College Marine Laboratory site (see photo) gave Laguna a bit of academic polish. Pomona College, an elite liberal arts school in the intimate *New England* tradition, is one of the Claremont Colleges. The laboratory continued in use until WWII. Standing behind the school is the office for Tent City, the alternative in those days to hotel lodging for students and visitors.

Isch Building (329-347 S. Coast): The first building on this site was the Isch Warling Palace Stable (a bed-and-breakfast for horses). The current building was named for Nick Isch and though he didn't build it, his family owned the building for many years. Take a look at the statue of Eiler Larsen, famous as the "Laguna Greeter." Eiler referred to this corner as his "office." (For more, see Chapter 21.)

Hotel Laguna (425 S. Coast) is a Laguna landmark and icon. Read about it in Chapter 3.

Wyland Studio Gallery (509 S. Coast) is home to Robert Wyland, the artist noted for his Whaling Walls (there's one on the north side). Wyland visited Laguna as a boy and the sight of migrating gray whales stirred something within. He returned in 1977 to paint them. The rest is history.

♥ **Brown's Park** (551 S. Coast) is a Laguna Beach treasure. The lot once contained a 2-level beach home with a prominent red brick chimney. Built in the '20s but owned by the Bergfeldt-Brown family since the '30s, the home was destroyed by giant swells during the 1998 El Nino storms. The Joseph E. Brown family generously donated the land to Laguna Beach for a park that future generations might also enjoy what they had treasured.

Orange Inn (703 S. Coast) isn't fancy but it's a genuine old Laguna hangout serving healthy food with a history dating to a highway stand in the 1920s. Locals like the egg dishes, muffins, and smoothies.

The Orange Inn—a favorite with locals as long as anyone can remember.
Photo: April Hellewell Dickson

WHITE HOUSE CAFE

What caused President Franklin D. Roosevelt's 1938 visit to tiny Laguna? Here's some background: Roosevelt was reelected in a 1936 landslide but overreached in his programs just as the Depression got worse and unemployment hit 20%. Some saw his liberal agenda and the growth of government as a burden on the economy. So the 1938-midterm congressional elections became a referendum on Roosevelt, a big worry for Democrats in office, and a reason to get out and visit the voters. Note the positioning of the White House Cafe. *Photo: First American, courtesy of the Laguna Beach Historical Society.*

DIRECTIONS: Cross Coast Highway at the Cleo St. crosswalk and head back (north).

Cottage Furnishings (802 S. Coast, one block south) offers coastal cottage charm in a furnishings shop that's become a local destination. Say hello to Louie Tarter, a Laguna character since '46.

The Collection at Laguna (540 S. Coast Hwy.) is a cluster of art galleries if you have time to look around.

Fong Imports (470 S. Coast) is a must see if you have any interest in Asian décor or collectables. Stop and meet the Fong family, on this block since '55.

Dilley's Books (460 S. Coast), founded by Jim and Jeanette Dilley, was once located in this 1930 Mission style building. Jim isn't around anymore but he was the genius that convinced a town to insulate itself from suburban sprawl by acquiring thousands of acres of surrounding land just to give it back to Nature. You can read more in Chapter 33 but for now, a reverent pause is in order.

Peppertree Lane (448 S. Coast) is a cluster of mini-shops around a charming walk-in lane, shaded by an old Peppertree. If you need some refreshment, try Gelato Paradiso, a favorite of locals. Surrounding Peppertree Lane are local eating spots, Tortilla Republic, Watermarc, and Nick's.

Heisler Building (Coast Hwy. at Laguna Ave.) was built in 1928 and recently had a total renovation done in a thoughtful nod to Laguna's history. In the beginning, Laguna Avenue was the business district and the first business, Nick Isch's grocery store and post office, stood on this corner. (See Chapter 1 for more on Howard Heisler.)

Fingerhut Gallery (Coast Hwy. at Forest Ave.) was once the Bank of America, and before that a popular lunch place, the Sandwich Mill. The Sandwich Mill is remembered for an afternoon gathering of creative guys called the "round table," organized by artist Frank Cuprien in the 1920s. Members of this daily meeting included Earl Stanly Gardner (famous for his Perry Mason novels), journalist Stan Chambers, and Hollywood people like Boris Karloff (a '30s superstar for his role as Frankenstein). According to Ramsey, "These men gave birth to the fame of Laguna Beach." (Source: *The First 100 Years in Laguna Beach*, Ramsey, 1976).

The White House (340 S. Coast) opened in 1918 as the White House Café and is Orange County's oldest restaurant. In 1915 the dirt road down Laguna Canyon was paved and Claude D. Bronner opened this restaurant in a newly built home. The opening of Coast Highway in 1926 caused a new surge of visitors and Richard Bird purchased the restaurant, adding the sign "Let the Birds feed you". Bird was a pioneer environmentalist. Lacking means to dispose of restaurant waste, he started a garbage company. Needing a way to process the garbage, he built a hog farm. When the manure began to pile up he sold it to local orange growers. There was very little waste. Today it offers food, drink, and DJ dancing, plus a great weekend brunch.

Laguna South Coast (162 S. Coast) America had a 20th century love affair with the silver screen and for Laguna it happened right here. Movies have been shown for nearly a century (1922-2015) in theatres built by the Aufdenkamp family. The original Lynn Theatre, subject to occasional flooding, was replaced by this building—complete with stage, orchestra pit, and murals by noted artist Edgar Payne—in 1933. Dedicated by Mary Pickford and Douglas Fairbanks, four generations of locals and visitors have been entertained by Hollywood storytellers in this building. At this writing the South Coast Theatre is silent—victim to the digital age—awaiting a new birth.

CHAPTER 6

Brooks and Cress Streets at Coast Highway

The Pottery Shack
1212 So. Coast Blvd. (U. S. 101
Laguna Beach, Calif.

DINNERWARE
ARTWARE
GARDENWARE

LARGEST STOCK
ON
PACIFIC COAST

"The Pottery Showplace of the Pacific Coast"

Laguna had an active ceramic trade between the two world wars that employed many artists. The Childs family opened this iconic shop at the peak of the pottery period, in 1936. It offered a vast collection of china and pottery in a colorful shop that was more like a bazaar. Under pressure from post-WWII imports the pottery shops disappeared but the Pottery Shack lasted into the 21st century. The building marks an important period of Laguna art history. Credit: *Tom Pulley Postcard Collection, courtesy of the Laguna Beach Historical Society.*

GETTING STARTED: This walk covers adjacent street corners on Coast Highway, so find parking around Brooks, or just walk the eight blocks from Main Beach. The walk starts at the English Garden florist shop on the northwest corner of Brooks and Coast Highway.

TIME: Allow one-half hour, or two hours if you like to shop.

The English Garden (1199 S. Coast) is a florist shop in a 1937 building with two tidbits of history: First, Aubrey St. Clair, known for his Mediterranean work, designed it in the English Tudor style. Second, this lovely building was actually the office for an early construction company—the Smith Brothers. It has seen many uses but remains our best Tudor Revival building. And a thought for the guys: It might help to buy your girl some flowers.

La Casa del Camino (1289 S. Coast) opened in 1928 and immediately became the hotel of choice. Movie actors stayed here during filming of the 1930 WWI blockbuster, *All Quiet on the Western Front.* The hotel is enjoying a revival and the Rooftop Lounge has become a popular nightspot. Because of the panoramic view of mountain and sea, it's said that both cougars and sharks can be seen on certain evenings.

Avila's El Ranchito (1305 S. Coast) is a good place to bring the kids and marks an important site: this was once the *Little Shrimp.* For three decades, until it closed in 1995, the Little Shrimp was the gay community's version of that TV sitcom bar "Cheers."

Friendship Shelter (1335 S. Coast), the Art Deco style building another 100 yards down Coast Highway, offers a heartwarming story. Laguna Beach has always been a welcoming place for people who are a little different. Think of the Laguna Greeter, a man who was not really well and had likely been run out of any number of towns in his travels. So it's fitting that homeless people are looked after and cared for in Laguna—just a few yards from beach homes priced in the millions.

The Friendship Shelter provides a home without charge, typically for 90 days, to homeless people and provides support services to help them achieve self-sufficiency and employment. The home has strict rules and retains 80% of any job wages to give back as a grubstake when their guests "graduate." If you're a praying person, ask the good Lord to watch over the Friendship Shelter.

DIRECTION: Cross Coast Hwy. at Cress and walk north.

Spencer Recovery Center (1316 S. Coast) provides drug rehab services. Built 1931 in Art Deco style, it later became the Hotel California. Do you remember the Eagle's 1976 hit song by the same name decrying a perceived decline into hedonism? Check the lyrics: "Such a lovely place, Such a lovely place... You can check out anytime you like, but you can never leave." Well there actually was a Hotel California, right here. The new mission of this old building seems appropriate.

The Old Pottery Place (1200 S. Coast) before its 2006 renovation was for many years the iconic Pottery Shack, which calls for a brief recounting of Laguna's now-forgotten ceramic art fame. It's one of our best-kept secrets and it all started nearby in the 1920s when Durlin Brayton, a Chicago Art Institute artist turned potter, designed the Hobbit-like cottage at 1450 S. Coast and began making colorful dinnerware.

Brayton, among Laguna's master artists, is believed to have innovated the fashion of simple earthenware dishes in vivid glaze colors (made possible by adding talc mined at Death Valley). He founded Brayton Laguna Pottery expanding on the land around his home. By the '40s over 150 artists worked night and day, making Brayton the "biggest gift and art pottery in the world." Many a down-on-their-luck artist found work decorating hand-painted ceramics. Laguna became a Mecca for potters, including Orville Kirby of Sleepy Hollow Pottery. (See "In the California Mold," *L.A. Times*, October 8, 1994.)

In 1936, sensing an opportunity, the Childs family opened the iconic Pottery Shack on this site, a factory and shop fashioned from beach cottages that prospered in the post-war years and became an international tourist attraction. (See postcard on page 27.) After WWII a flood of inexpensive imports from Japan and Italy sent Laguna's pottery industry into decline. (Braytons closed in 1968.)

The Pottery Shack was the last survivor of Laguna's famed potters and has been tastefully restored by the Hanauer family into today's *Old Pottery Place*, offering Sapphire Laguna (a restaurant and pantry), Chocolate Soldier (handmade confections), Laguna Beach Books (to this writer's knowledge, the last of Orange County's neighborhood, full-service bookstores), and other shops. You're standing in a historic place—take a moment to enjoy the art preserved here.

Heidelberg Pastry Bistro (1100 S. Coast) marks the end of the walk. It's a warm, inviting place to relax and enjoy a pastry or beverage. You've earned it.

If you have some time:

Thalia Street at 900 S. Coast Highway: This corner, 2 blocks north, shouldn't be overlooked. You can rent a bike at **Laguna Cyclery** (240 Thalia) or get a bite at **The Stand,** a source of healthy snacks for locals since the early '70s. Thalia Beach marks the surfers' zone, as evidenced by shops across the street: Second Reef Surf Shop and Thalia Surf Shop.

CHAPTER 7

Aliso Creek Canyon and Beach

Aerial view of Montage Laguna Beach with Treasure Island (formerly Goff Island) in the foreground. *Photo: Courtesy of Montage Laguna Beach.*

GETTING STARTED: From Main Beach, head south on Coast Highway for 2.5 miles to:

• Montage Laguna Beach, 30801 S. Coast (turn right on Shreve Dr. for valet parking, or continue to Wesley Dr. and take the ramp right to underground public parking). You can enjoy refreshments at the 5-star Montage resort, sunbath at Treasure Island Beach, or enjoy an evening walk on the bluff (Laguna's best sunset view).

• The Ranch (31106 S. Coast, continue ¼ mile south, turn left on Village Lane and continue ¼ mile to free parking). Once the Thurston Homestead, reborn as the Ranch offering golf, hotel, and food in the beauty of Aliso Canyon.

• Aliso Beach Park (continue south on Coast Hwy and you can't miss it.) This is the best beach for convenient parking, available on both sides of the highway.

The Early Homesteads

George and Sarah Thurston—Laguna's first homesteaders—settled on Aliso Creek in 1871 and begin to farm, though it was a hardscrabble existence. Their son Joe Thurston took over the farm but in the '30s he moved into town. Joe left behind a charming memoir—*Laguna Beach of Early Days*. (For more see Chapter 28.)

The Goff family arrived around 1876 and two brothers, Frank and Lee, homesteaded along the coast north and south of the Thurston farm. Though the coast was scenic, the limited water supply made farming difficult. The Goffs raised potatoes on the bluff where the Montage resort is now; crops ripened early due to the temperate weather gaining a good price at market. They also raised barley and hauled it to San Diego on the schooner *Emma*, anchored near their Goff Island pier. (For more see Chapter 30)

Girl Scout Camp

In the early 1900s two heiress sisters, Florence and Blanche Dolph, came to southern California and began to invest in South Laguna property, including the Goff homesteads (see above). Their holding included the coastal area developed as Lagunita and Coast Royal in the '20s. In 1935 they donated two acres in Aliso Canyon (adjoining the old Moulton Ranch) for a Girl Scout camp that was used into the 1970s. Girls of that era have fond memories of camping in Aliso Canyon. The land, despite stipulations in the deed, was later diverted to other uses. (See "Heiresses Leave a Lasting Heritage: a Scout Camp", by Ann Christoph, *The Indy*, 18 May 2008.)

Beach Camping

In 1920 George Wesley Wilson settled in Laguna and opened a store—the Aliso View Grocery—on the bluff overlooking Aliso Beach. (Wesley Drive, and Wilson Avenue remember him today.)   The Wilsons also operated a tent and trailer camp on Aliso Beach. The area became a Mecca for campers when Pacific Coast Highway replaced the single-lane dirt road along the coast in '26, and the Goff Island Trailer Camp opened on the bluff above Goff Island.

The movie *Treasure Island*, based on Robert Louis Stevenson's classic novel, was filmed around Goff Island in '34 so later, when permanent trailer sites were developed on the bluff (upgrading the "camp" to a "park"), the name changed to Treasure Island Trailer Park. The improvements were sufficient that the '54 blockbuster comedy starring Lucile Ball and Desi Arnaz, *The Long, Long Trailer,* was filmed starting its journey from the park. Several generations of beach lovers kept trailers at the park—it was an idyllic but affordable way to have a home by the sea. But as the decades passed, decline and decay turned the camp into an eyesore.

Montage Laguna Beach

The decaying trailer park was a natural site for a resort hotel but as the years rolled by nothing happened. Finally a workable plan was approved and Montage Laguna Beach resort opened in 2003. Land was set aside for Treasure Island Park, thus restoring public access to four pristine beaches. Montage is a world-class resort designed in the Green Brother's Craftsman style complete with paintings by early Laguna Impressionists. Montage, perched on land the Franklin Goff family homesteaded in the 1870s, enhances the fame of Laguna Beach.

The Ranch at Laguna Beach

The Thurston family farmed their homestead for two generations until son Joe sold it and moved into town. (In the 1930 Census his occupation changed from farmer to realtor). Bill Bryant acquired most of the farm in the '40s envisioning a golf course resort, which became the grandly named Laguna Beach Country Club—a name at odds with Laguna's artsy vibe. Ben and Violet Brown took over in 1956 and after his death Violet renamed it the Aliso Creek Inn and Golf Course, naming the restaurant after her late husband. Violet persevered through the occasional flooding of Aliso Creek, finally selling in 2004.

Though just nine holes, it was a magical place for golf. With the exception of the fairways the rugged canyon remained largely unchanged, serenely quiet, a home to deer that grazed when the golfers had departed. (The site of the old Thurston farmhouse is near the 3rd green.) With the passage of time the property deteriorated but things picked up when Mark Christy and local investors took over in 2014, envisioning a premier coastal resort with a legacy name: *The Ranch at Laguna Beach*. The inn has been remodeled to 95 rooms and cottages; the golf course carries the legacy name, *Ben Brown's Golf Course at The Ranch at Laguna Beach*; the restaurant is renamed *Harvest*; and a new spa will be named *Sycamore Spa*.

Aliso Creek Canyon and the fairways of Ben Brown's Golf Course at The Ranch, looking towards the ocean. *Photo: Courtesy of The Ranch at Laguna Beach.*

THE COTTAGES OF LAGUNA (AND A CASTLE)

Back in 1987 a local girl published a remarkable book, *The Cottages & Castles of Laguna: Historic Architecture 1883-1940*. Karen Wilson Turnbull is the author; her Laguna origins go back to 1920 when grandfather George Wesley Wilson drove down the coast on a single-lane dirt road to settle in South Laguna. *Photo: David Laws*

George opened "The Aliso View Grocery" and developed a camping park on Aliso Beach. Granddaughter Karen worked on the Laguna Beach Historic Survey of older building and sketched the most interesting buildings for her book. She takes little credit, but the book was a local bestseller, created a public appreciation for our architectural heritage, and is now a collectible. Much credit for the next four chapters goes to Karen Wilson Turnbull, and those who worked on the Historic Survey project. (For more on the Wilson family of south Laguna, visit light-headed.com.)

CHAPTER 8

The Three Oldest Homes

If you're short of time and can't visit the homes shown in Chapters 9, 10, and 11, here is a quick 30-minute drive-by tour of Laguna's three oldest homes.

GETTING STARTED: An important courtesy—these homes have historic interest but they are private homes; please do not trespass or disturb the residents. All directions start from Main Beach (the intersection of Broadway with Coast Highway). The homes are presented in order of age.

DIRECTIONS TO 154 PEARL STREET: From Main Beach, go south on Coast Highway 1.2 miles and turn right on Agate Street. At the bottom of Agate turn left on Ocean Way and continue to the end—the Harper Home is on your left.

The Harper Home (154 Pearl St.)

This newly renovated board-and-batten cottage was built in 1883 from driftwood and lumber floated ashore from boats. Thomas Harper, the early Laguna architect, lived here as a child. (For more on Harper see Chapter 12.)

DIRECTIONS TO 411 ARROYO CHICO: From Pearl Street turn left on Coast Hwy. and continue left 0.8 miles to Cleo St. Turn right on Cleo and continue two blocks to Catalina St., then veer right onto Arroyo Chico. The Captain's Home is on the SE corner.

The Captain's Home (411 Arroyo Chico)

In the late 1800s good money was being made in citrus so successful growers had the means to escape the summer heat. Riverside families were the first to build beach homes, starting along the bluff south of the Hotel Laguna. Captain Benjamin Handy built this 1884 home, Laguna's only remaining Victorian, on the bluff near the bottom of Legion Street. It was relocated to this site in the 1970s.

From *Cottages and Castles of Laguna*: "Built in the pioneer Victorian style, it features a jig-sawn bargeboard (the decorative gable face) and ornamental railings. There is a tall, vertical format to the house as is typical of the style. The redwood lumber was hauled through Laguna Canyon by mule."

Captain Benjamin Handy Residence (411 Arroyo Chico). *Credit: Sketch from The Cottages and Castles of Laguna, courtesy Karen Wilson Turnbull.*

DIRECTIONS TO 412 GLENNEYRE ST: Use the turning circle at end of Arroyo Chico and take Catalina Street north (towards downtown) to the end, which is Park Avenue. As you pass Legion Street note the Legion Hall, built in 1908 as a two-room schoolhouse. At Park Avenue admire the two churches. (See Chapter 31.) Turn left on Park Avenue and as you approach Glenneyre note the red home on the SE corner.

The Cope House (412 Glenneyre)

A colony for English Immigrants was started in today's Lake Forest in the 1880s; prospective settlers were enticed by the 1893 book, *Fruit Farming for Profit in California*, published in London. The first Englishman was S. H. Cope, actually in the area since 1888 (according to Clara M. Fox's *A History of El Toro*). Cope, a carpenter, purchased some land and built an El Toro home. He did well enough to build this 1897 Laguna summer home on a one-acre lot with a barn across the street. The embankment was created when the streets were paved.

DIRECTIONS: Continue down (Park Ave. becomes Laguna Ave.) to Coast Highway and turn right to the starting point at Main Beach.

NORTH LAGUNA
COTTAGE TOUR

Crescent Bay Dr

Hillcrest Dr

Fairview St

Wave St

Beverly St

Cliff Dr

Hawthorne Dr

High Dr

Myrtle St

Pacific Coast Highway

Locust St

Jasmine St

Aster St

Cedar Way

START
HERE

Broadway St

Main
Beach

CHAPTER 9

North Laguna Cottages

In the beginning, north Laguna was part of the San Joaquin Rancho, then the Irvine Ranch in 1876. James Irvine sold this portion of his ranch in 1905 to Howard Heisler and partners. They set land aside for Heisler Park along the bluff top, subdivided the rest, and piped in water from Laguna Canyon. Laguna Beach was difficult to reach in the horse-and-buggy era but Henry Ford mass-produced Model Ts starting in 1908 and that changed everything. To encourage building on sold lots, Heisler offered a $100 prize for the first home built and the first residence on this tour won the prize.

Though eight homes are featured on this tour, you'll pass other charming residences. Please drive carefully; the streets can be narrow, often without sidewalks, and are shared with humans and pets. The drive takes ½ to 1 hour. Bring a picnic lunch if you want to stop along the way.

DIRECTIONS: From Main Beach head north on Coast Hwy 0.3 mile and turn right on Jasmine St. Go one block to Magnolia and check the cottage set back on the far right (southeast) corner.

Jasmine & 390 Magnolia St: A family built (or assembled; Sears used to sell kits) this Settlement style home over one weekend in 1907 with the help of friends. They won a $100 prize for the first home built in Laguna Cliffs, plus bragging rights to north Laguna's oldest home.

DIRECTION: Continue ¼ block to 416 Jasmine (on the left).

Cotswold cottage at 416 Jasmine. *Credit: Sketch from The Cottages and Castles of Laguna, courtesy Karen Wilson Turnbull.*

416 Jasmine St: This charming home is Laguna's best example of an English Cotswold cottage. The entry turret with its round-topped, rough-hewn door is typical of this fairy-tale style.

DIRECTION: Drive to the end of Jasmine Street and turn left on High Drive. Continue three blocks and look on the right for 568 High Drive.

568 High Drive: This charming steeply gabled home features a wonderful view of the coast and has delightful grounds. The home was built in 1922.

DIRECTIONS: When you come to the ravine (called Boat Canyon), turn right on Hillcrest Drive. Continue to #770, on the right. (Note: Tall hedges cover the front but there's a view up the driveway.)

Pyne Castle, 770 Hillcrest: A century ago Walter Pyne jumped on the emerging digital technology of his time: player pianos. He owned the Orange County franchise; his brother had Los Angeles. Pyne invested his gains in a Santa Ana Canyon orange farm where, fortuitously, oil was discovered so his wealth increased. Pyne, an eccentric character, then purchased a row of lots in Laguna in the 1920s and built this Norman style mansion. He willed the 62-room mansion to his housekeeper (she had earned it; he was a difficult character), and at her death to the Christian Science Church. It was later converted to condominium apartments.

DIRECTIONS: Continue up Hillcrest Drive, turn left on Wave St. and look for a place to park.

Witch's House, 290 Wave Street: This really should be the *Hansel and Gretel* house but another home has that title (see Chapter 10). This picturesque home was the dream of Whittier carpenter Vernon Barker who designed and built it in the late '20s. Note how Barker was capable of both Disneyland-quality creativity, and masterly craftsmanship. History doesn't record what his wife thought of all this. There's an interesting renovation project next door at #274.

DIRECTIONS: Continue down Wave to Coast Hwy and turn right. After six blocks look for Crescent Bay Dr., turning left to #147:

147 Crescent Bay: This 1936 home is somewhat obscured by the plants but has noteworthy architecture. Architect Aubrey St. Clair was known for his Mediterranean revival public buildings but he also designed this Moderne style home. The Moderne style was popular in the '30s, but 77 years later it still looks contemporary.

The Witch's House (290 Wave Street). *Credit: Sketch from The Cottages and Castles of Laguna, courtesy Karen Wilson Turnbull.*

183 Crescent Bay: It's a little squeezed by neighboring homes but this is Laguna's best example of classic Spanish Colonial design. The home would fit right in when Spain ruled California.

Crescent Bay Point Park: As long as you're in the area, stop to admire the view from this picturesque park. If you brought a lunch, this is the place to enjoy it.

DIRECTIONS: If you have time, follow Crescent Bay Dr. back to Coast Hwy. and turn right (towards Main Beach). Turn right on Fairview St. (the 4th right turn) and park near 989 Cliff Dr.

989 Cliff Drive: To appreciate this home, take the parallel public stairway down to Shaw's Cove. This beautiful Early California Mission style villa was built in 1928, and features private beach access and boat storage. Extra glamour point: It's a former home of actress Diane Keaton.

DIRECTIONS: This is the end of the tour of north Laguna historic homes. Continue down Cliff Dr. to Coast Highway and your starting point at Main Beach.

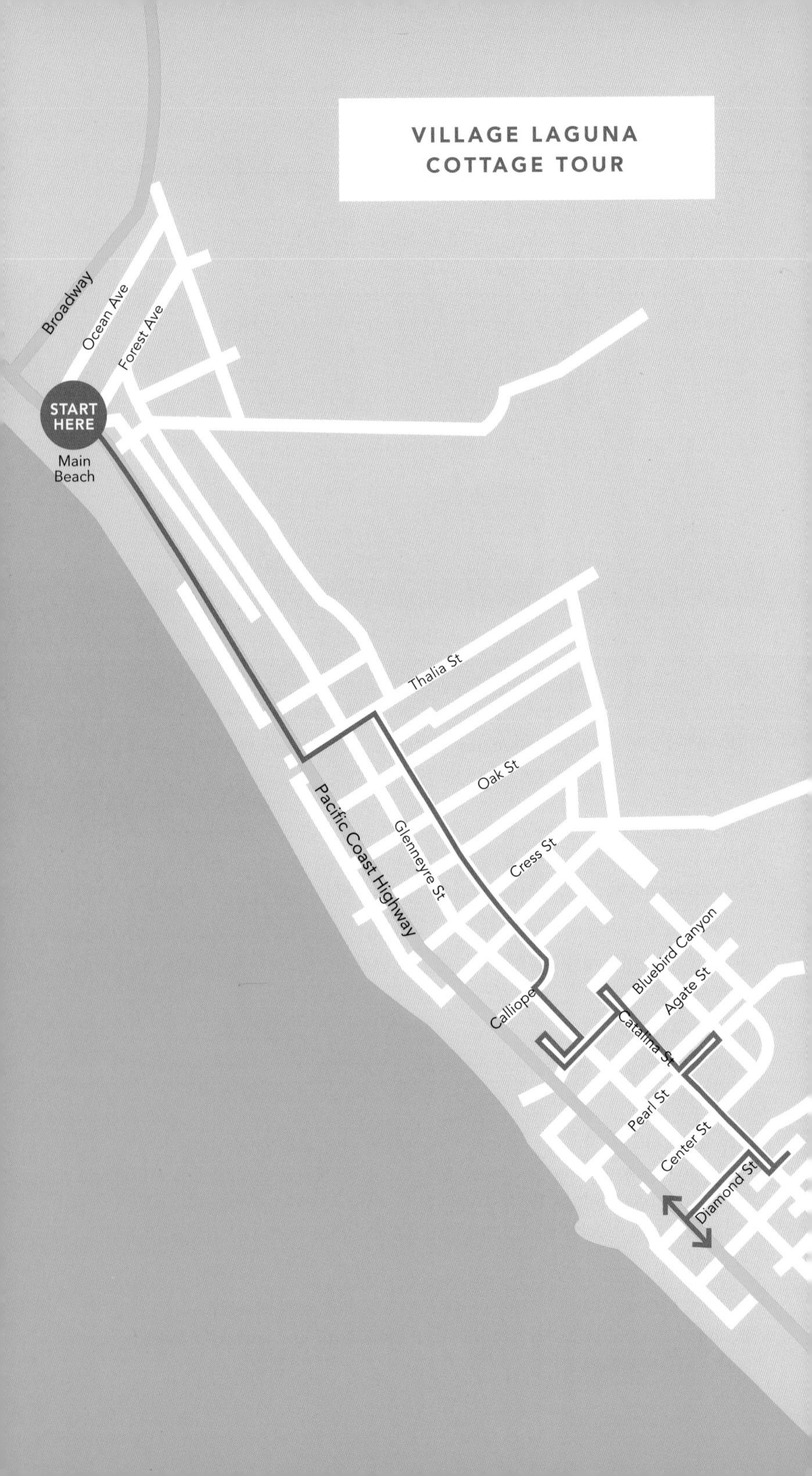

VILLAGE LAGUNA
COTTAGE TOUR

START
HERE
Main
Beach

Broadway
Ocean Ave
Forest Ave

Thalia St

Oak St

Pacific Coast Highway

Glenneyre St

Cress St

Calliope

Bluebird Canyon

Agate St

Catalina St

Pearl St

Center St

Diamond St

CHAPTER 10

Village Laguna Cottages

Village Laguna refers to the area between Laguna Canyon and Bluebird Canyon (south Laguna is the area below Nyes Place/Victoria Beach). This is a tour of six historic Laguna homes along Catalina Avenue, and leads to the four Moss Point homes of Chapter 11. There are other picturesque residences along the way. Please drive carefully; the streets often lack sidewalks and are shared with humans and pets.

DIRECTIONS: From Main Beach head south on Coast Hwy. about 1 mile; turn left on Thalia and then right on Catalina St. Continue to 1173 Catalina.

1173 Catalina: Though a little hidden by trees and vines, the steep roof, leaded windows, and stone chimney of this 1929 home could easily be found in England. This area of Village Laguna contains many charming cottages from the '20s.

DIRECTIONS: Continue south on Catalina to the end where it swings right to Calliope St. Take Calliope and make three quick turns: left on Glenneyre, right on Bluebird Canyon, and right on Galen Street.

A classic California Craftsman home; 1560 Galen Drive. *Credit: Sketch from The Cottages and Castles of Laguna, courtesy Karen Wilson Turnbull.*

1560 Galen: Built by Laguna Lumber worker Floyd Case, later the city's first building inspector, this 1929 Craftsman style home displays beautiful design and workmanship (though nearby commercial buildings have encroached).

DIRECTIONS: There is place to turn around at the bottom of Galen. Return up Bluebird Canyon to Catalina Dr. Turn left on Catalina and look for #1559.

1559 Catalina: This is another of Laguna's dream homes (meaning creative rather than simply expensive). Built in 1930 by H. L. Hamaker, a cabinetmaker and artist, this could easily have been Hansel and Gretel's residence.

The Hansel and Gretel home (1559 Catalina). *Credit: Sketch from The Cottages and Castles of Laguna, courtesy Karen Wilson Turnbull.*

DIRECTIONS: Continue south on Catalina three blocks to Pearl Street and turn left, to 489 Pearl.

Enchanted House (489 Pearl St.), was once the home of movie director Malcolm St. Clair. From 1917 to 1945 St. Clair made almost 100 films, including the first (1928) *Gentlemen Prefer Blonds*. St. Clair also acted, though he was 6'-7" tall.

DIRECTIONS: Return down Pearl to Catalina and turn left. Continue three blocks to Osgood Court. This is a narrow street so parking on Catalina and walking might be easier. See 470 Osgood Ct.

470 Osgood Ct: A fence hides the home, one of four remaining by Carl Abel, but the hand-carved garage door is the main feature. Abel was a Danish homebuilder remembered by his handsome woodcarvings. (See Chapter 12 for sketch.)

DIRECTIONS: Head back down Osgood Ct. and turn right on Catalina. Take Catalina one block to Diamond and turn left to #290 (on the right).

The Warling home is a link to the earliest pioneer families. *Credit: Sketch from The Cottages and Castles of Laguna, courtesy Karen Wilson Turnbull.*

Warling Home (290 Diamond): This early Craftsman style cottage, built 1906 at the corner of Forest and Coast Highway (Pacific Avenue back then) was the home of Laguna pioneers Oscar and Ora Warling. The Warlings owned much downtown property (she was the niece of George Rogers who subdivided the downtown area). The 1932 widening of Coast Highway caused their home to be moved here.

DIRECTIONS: Continue down Diamond to Coast Highway. To visit historic Moss Point (see Chapter 11) turn left on Coast for two blocks then right on Moss Street. Look for a place to park. To end the tour, turn right on Coast Highway and return to Main Beach starting point.

Four Historic Moss Point Homes

The first home on Moss Point was built in 1905. That residence was moved to the back of the lot about 1917 to make way for this home, built by the brother of Colonel House. At the time the "highway" was a dirt road. Colonel House was a key supporter of President Woodrow Wilson and Wilson once convalesced here. *Credit: Sketch from The Cottages and Castles of Laguna, courtesy Karen Wilson Turnbull.*

The intersection of Moss Street with Ocean Way features four homes that could each qualify for the register of historic homes. Take the steps down to Moss Street Beach to appreciate why the Moss Point-Woods Cove area was hot during the 1920s boom era.

DIRECTIONS: This is the continuation of Chapter 10. If you are starting fresh, take Coast Hwy south from Main Beach for 1.6 miles and turn right at Moss St. Look for a place to park. Going clockwise from the oldest on the SE quadrant:

2241 S. Coast: The upper home was first located out on Moss Point in 1905 and then relocated to this site about 1917 to make way for the Col. House residence. This is one of the best pre-1920 homes built along the bluff when Coast Highway was a single-lane dirt road.

Col. House Estate (139 Moss): This home, somewhat hidden by the garage, sits on a majestic site with historic importance. Col. House was instrumental in the reelection of Woodrow Wilson, and the president once convalesced in this home. It was built in 1917 and features both Craftsman and Cape Cod style design elements; the architect is unknown.

The Ark (2191 Ocean): Long owned by a Wrigley heir, this funky 1925 home was designed by the architect Jean Egasse to resemble a boat, thus its name. You could count on Egasse not to be boring.

2192 Ocean: This 1927 residence is Laguna's best example of a Craftsman home, the style developed by Pasadena architects Charles and Henry Green. The style emphasizes shingled exterior walls, overhanging rooflines with exposed beams, native materials, and arts and crafts details. In this era sunshine and fresh air were considered healthy so Green Brothers homes featured clusters of vertical windows and covered sleeping porches on the second level. *Credit: Sketch from The Cottages and Castles of Laguna, courtesy Karen Wilson Turnbull.*

DIRECTIONS: Continue up Ocean Way three blocks to Pearl Street; it's an interesting drive. Diamond Street marks the entrance to Woods Cove, much painted by artist Robert Wood. The "Bette Davis home," 1991 Ocean Way, was home to the noted actress in the '40s. The corner cottage at the end of Pearl is Laguna's oldest. Turn right on Pearl to Coast Highway, then left on Coast back to Main Beach.

CHAPTER 12

The Early Architects

The bane of architects and builders is the cyclical nature of their business—it's either boom or bust. Life was quiet after the bust in the 1890s, but in 1915 business picked up as they paved the dirt road down Laguna Canyon, dedicated Coast Highway in 1926, and incorporated the city in 1927.

You could see the growth in the school system: In the early years the kids in Laguna met in a single class. In 1908, when a new building was needed, the town optimistically built a two-room school but the second room sat empty for years. There was still just one class when Doc Blacketer enrolled in 1923. But by 1927 the school was nearing 200 students and a new classroom was needed every year. The sudden growth came from film people who fell in love with Laguna when shooting movies, but artists were also moving here. *(Source: Jones, 2003)*

Laguna was fortunate to have three unusually skilled architects during this period: Aubrey St. Clair, Thomas Harper, and Jean Egasse. Also notable is Carl Abel, Danish-born designer and wood carver who came in 1937. The Abel family has designed and built homes in Laguna ever since.

Aubrey St. Clair's father kicked off the art colony after he painted here in 1900 and displayed his watercolors in San Francisco. Like his father, Aubrey was an architect who enjoyed art. St. Clair did most of the public buildings, the water department, firehouse, city hall, sewage plant, town library, El Morro School, as well as the library and cafeteria at the high school. He typically designed Mediterranean revival buildings, as can be seen by a walk up Forest Avenue (see Chapter 4). However St. Clair also designed in the Moderne style: the 147 Crescent Bay residence, built in 1936, still looks contemporary after more than 75 years.

Thomas Harper, like St. Clair, had deep roots in Laguna—he grew up in the oldest remaining residence. The family home at 154 Pearl was built in 1883 using driftwood and wood floated in from ships. Harper traveled Europe in the '20s but returned to Laguna in time for the building boom. He is best known for his Period Revival cottages such as the 1926 Rose Cottage (631 Virginia Park Dr.), the Manzanita Cottages (732 Manzanita), the expansion of Villa Rockledge, and the eclectic shingled home on the bluff in Sleepy Hollow (seen on the Main Beach Walk in Chapter 2).

Jean (or Yann) Egasse born 1886 in Paris, France, apprenticed at landscape during the *garden city* movement in England, before immigrating to California. Though not formally trained in architecture, during his five brief years in Laguna (c. 1925-1930) he graced our town with five buildings of unusual charm. The Jahraus family commissioned two Norman Revival style buildings on Forest Avenue (#305, the old Eschbach's Florist, and #384, still known as the Lumberyard), with hopes other buildings would follow. This didn't happen but Egasse also designed a *storybook* cottage (1280 N. Coast Hwy.) known as "The Castle", showing his ability to integrate building and landscape. The *Ark* is a whimsical ship-like Craftsman home overlooking Moss Point (see Chapter 11).

The Abel Family: A discussion of Laguna architects would be incomplete without mentioning the Abel family. Four generations have contributed to architecture and art in Laguna. The first, Carl Abel, came in 1937 and four of his picturesque homes remain. A good example of his woodcarving skill is 470 Osgood Ct. (see below).

Carl's son Mogens left woodcarvings about the city also and for years played Judas in the last scene of the Pageant; his son Chris was a noted Laguna artist and architect. In the 3rd generation, Gregg is a noted architect (note the renovation of the Lumberyard on Forest), and Lark is a glass carver. From the 4th generation, artist Tristan preserves the tradition of woodcarving, and Lea is an artist and director at Anneliese School. *(Sources: Gregg Abel; also "The Abel Legacy," L. B. Independent, 11 Nov. 2011.)*

Credit: *The Cottages and Castles of Laguna, courtesy Karen Wilson Turnbull.*

Pavilion, Laguna, Cal.

HOW THE ARTISTS SAVED LAGUNA

Instead of a charming art colony known for early California impressionists, Laguna could just as easily have become one of those kitschy beach towns. You know, with tattoo parlors... well actually, we do have Laguna Tattoo, said to be the oldest in Orange County. But you get the point—Laguna could have turned out much worse. So in this section we tell how the artists saved Laguna.

In Chapter 13, architect and artist Norman St. Clair discovers Laguna and spreads the word. Soon there were a string of studios along the coast and the old Pavilion was converted to a gallery to show their work. To operate the gallery the Laguna Beach Art Association (Orange County's first cultural organization) was founded and a dedicated fireproof art gallery and museum was built (the first in southern California). On the topic of art, a lot of "firsts" happened in Laguna.

AT LEFT: The "Pavilion," Laguna's first town hall, was built in 1908 with funds from Riverside families who wished to hold Sunday services. As the signs show, it worked equally well for dances. Later moved to Graceland Drive it became the home of artist and pianist Fred Swankowsky. *Credit: First American photo, courtesy of the Laguna Beach Historical Society.*

Chapter 14 tells how Laguna's starving but resourceful artists expanded the market for their art by first organizing a Festival of Arts, and then a Pageant of The Masters. The Pageant, which presents noted artworks using live actors, is now world famous.

In Chapter 15 five of Laguna's early artists are remembered. Finally, in Chapter 16, we take a walk through Laguna's three gallery districts. "

CHAPTER 13
An Art Colony Forms

The First Artists: Norman St. Clair, Los Angeles architect turned artist, first came to Laguna by train and stagecoach to paint in 1900. His watercolors created a stir when exhibited in San Francisco. This drew noted painters Granville Redmond, Elmer and Marion Kavanaugh Wachtel, and then Gardner Symons. Symons brought William Wendt here on a painting trip, camping in an abandoned farmhouse. Symons bought a home in Arch Beach in 1903 and then enticed William Swift Daniell to Laguna. Wendt, who spent much of his career in Laguna even though his sculptress wife Julia Bracken worked in Los Angeles, invited Guy Rose to paint here. Rose and Wendt were considered the two premier southern California painters of the early 1900s (Gerdts, William H., *American Impressionism*, 1984).

Conway Griffith settled in Arch Beach in 1908 and Frank Cuprien built his Viking studio on an ocean bluff in 1912. The Bohemian atmosphere at the Viking made it a gathering place for artists, and Cuprien, a former opera singer, was crowned "dean of the art colony." Artist Anna Hills came in 1913, stayed the rest of her life, and became a vital force in the community.

And in this way an important artist colony developed amidst the villages that grew into Laguna Beach. The L. A. Times art critic visited in 1906 and returned in 1915. He marveled how in those nine years the number of artists working in Laguna had swelled from a handful to over 35, with a string of studios reaching from Arch Beach up to Laguna Cliffs (north Laguna).

The First Gallery: Edgar and Elsie Payne, both excellent artists, arrived in 1917. Edgar was an exceptional organizer; in 1918 he rallied the artists to open the first art galley in a renovated community hall remembered as the "Pavilion." Twenty-five painters exhibited their work and many visitors came. From this success the Laguna Beach Art Association was formed with Payne as president. Just 35 of the LBAA's 150 charter members were artists, so there was broad community support (the populations was scarcely 300, counting children).

Frank Cuprien described the community spirit: "We fixed up the ramshackle old building with the assistance of Nick Isch. First we drove the bats out of the building and built a skylight in the roof. We whitewashed the walls and oiled the floors . . . . Everybody worked like Trojans." You can see a miniature model of that first gallery in the Laguna Art Museum, complete with figures of the artists. *(Source: LagunaArtMuseum.org.)*

The Museum: Edgar Payne then envisioned a larger, permanent gallery to properly exhibit art and left Anna Hills in charge while he took an extended painting trip. Hills was up to the task; Howard Heisler gave the LBAA a deal on some prime property and in 1929 southern California's first dedicated public gallery—today's Laguna Art Museum—opened at 307 Cliff Dr. This was a remarkable achievement for a town of just 2000 people; much had been accomplished in the first three decades of the 20th century.

The original mission was to serve as a permanent gallery, displaying paintings by local artists for sale. But as the early artists began to die a memorial collection was started. The work of other artists was collected, beginning in 1966. There were private galleries in Laguna but in the '60s they increased in importance, and a few artists groups organized their own galleries, not unlike the original LBAA. Eventually, in 1972, it made sense that the Laguna Beach Art Association—the oldest cultural organization in Orange County—be renamed the Laguna Beach Museum of Art. The metamorphosis from the people's gallery to the people's museum was complete. (Source: "75 Works, 75 Years, Collecting the Art of California: The Years 1918-1955," by art historian Nancy Dustin Wall Moure.)

CHAPTER 14

Festival of Arts and Pageant of the Masters

Entrance to the Festival of Arts and Pageant of the Masters, located at 650 Laguna Canyon Road. *Photo: Skip Hellewell*

The automobile changed everything for Laguna. The Model T Ford, America's first affordable car, was introduced in 1908. In 1915 the dirt road down Laguna Canyon was paved. In 1926 the Pacific Coast Highway reached Laguna (though in Laguna it's called "Coast Highway"). These changes made it possible for Santa Ana, Anaheim, Riverside, Los Angeles and even Pasadena people to weekend in Laguna. If you owned a car you wanted to take a ride so what better place than the beach, especially on the 4th of July.

Like the land boom of the 1880s, there was a housing boom in the 1920s. These booms, like our own recent real estate bubble, seem to come along each generation. The real estate boom of the '20s peaked in 1926-27; many of Laguna's downtown buildings date to that period. Trailing the real estate boom there was a sharp stock market boom that collapsed on Black Friday, 1929. The nation slowly sank into the Great Depression of the '30s and—unfortunately for our art colony—few suffer more in a bad economy that the artists.

The 1932 Olympics were held in Los Angeles and the starving artists of Laguna got the idea to lure those wealthy enough to attend to come down to Laguna and buy some art. The Festival of Art is the result of that first effort.

The **Festival of Arts** was a creative means of connecting artists with art collectors. The first festival in 1932 was held on El Paseo, the short street by the Hotel Laguna. The community joined in an advertising campaign to get out the word and the show was a success. The festival moved around for a few years until the present site was secured at 650 Laguna Canyon Road. The selection of artists for the Festival is by jury; within the art community it's an honor to be selected.

There had been a community outdoor play in Laguna promoted by Isaac Frazee, called the Peace Pipe Pageant but a new show took its place. For the second Festival of Arts, vaudeville actress and artist Lolita Perine organized the townspeople to portray paintings in a living art show, or *tableaux vivant*. Though simply done, it was an immediate hit so was repeated in following years.

The **Pageant of The Masters** grew out of this living show when Roy and Marie Ropp, he a local developer, were assigned to make improvements. The show grew in sophistication, always using volunteer townspeople as actors. The Pageant has continued ever since, except during WWII.

The theme of the show changes each year. Though the art is constantly changing, the final scene is traditionally Leonardo da Vinci's "The Last Supper." Here is Roy Ropp's description of the first close with this painting (Gibby, 1966):

> *A reverent silence spread over the audience. Stillness was complete. A brief narration—then the curtain slowly opened as the rich baritone voice of Mr. John Ferguson sang the beautiful Lord's Prayer by Alfred Hay Malott, gradually building up to the great climax. The curtain remained open for a time, that the picture might be seen in complete silence—then it slowly closed upon this great drama.*

> *The audience was profoundly enthralled. They had experienced a sacrament, a great benediction. Immediate conversation seemed impossible. Thus ended the first program in the second year of the Pageant of the Masters.*

The **Sawdust Art Festival** (originally the Laguna Artists and Gallery Owners Association) broke away from the Festival of Arts in 1965 due to differences over the jury system. The Sawdust is now a short walk past the Festival grounds, at 935 Laguna Canyon Road. The name came from the practice of sprinkling wood chips on the ground to keep the dust down.

Sawdust presents the work of over 200 Laguna Beach artists, including "demo" booths (my favorite is the glass blower). There are also booths for young people to be taught art techniques (a hit with children). This is an art show for and by the artists—the governing board is taken from exhibiting artists and each year the artists set up and decorate their own booth before the sawdust is spread. It's an informal, free-spirited event.

The **Laguna Playhouse** was an early presence in the Art Colony. Perhaps it was the success of the first community art gallery in 1918, but in 1920 today's Laguna Playhouse was organized and in 1924 a new community building at 319 Ocean Ave. provided facilities for shows. The city assumed ownership during the Depression to save the playhouse from closure. The Playhouse was used for USO shows during WWII.

The South Coast Repertory Theatre soldiered on after the war and in 1969, helped by a gift from Nellie Gail Moulton, the Moulton Theatre was built on city land at 606 Laguna Canyon Road, adjacent to Festival of Arts grounds. The Laguna Playhouse—billed as the West Coast's oldest continuous repertory theatre—is alive and well, after nearly a century.

The **Art School of Laguna** began as a joint venture of the Laguna Beach Art Association and Festival of Arts in 1962, a natural progression from the schools offered by artists like Anna Hills. The school was successful but nonprofit status was denied due to its ties with the LBAA. So it 1964 the Art School became independent and continues today as the Laguna College of Art and Design with its campus at 2222 Laguna Canyon Road.

CHAPTER 15

Five Artists

Many, many artists have worked in Laguna but we should remember the notables of the original colony:

Frank Cuprien –
– Pioneer Artist

Frank Cuprien had a studio called the Viking on the bluff in Arch Beach; he left his estate to the Laguna Art Museum. *Credit: First American, courtesy of the Laguna Beach Historical Society.*

Frank Cuprien (1871-1948), musician and artist, studied at Cooper Union Art School and in Europe, then taught at Baylor University before settling in Laguna Beach in 1913, the year several gifted artists arrived. He built a rustic home and studio called the "Viking" on an Arch Beach bluff, which became a Bohemian gathering place for artists. He continued to use lanterns and cook by fire long after electricity came to Laguna. Cuprien was president of the Art Association, 1921-22, to which he bequeathed his estate and art collection. A plaque at 1603 S. Coast Hwy marks the site of the "Viking".

Anna Althea Hills (1882-1930) studied at the Art Institute of Chicago, traveled in Europe, then made Laguna her home. She opened a studio, and became a vital force in the community. The Laguna Art Museum was built during her tenure as president of the Art Association. Hills also conducted an art school for children in the summers. In Laguna she painted colorful landscapes and marine subjects with a post-Impressionist style in watercolor and oil.

A founding member of the Presbyterian Church in Laguna, she wrote its history. Her passing at a relatively young age was much mourned; a plaque at the art museum she helped to build remembers her.

Edgar Payne (1883-1947) was perhaps the best known of the Early California *plein air* artists. Though he painted in many areas, including the Four Corners area and the Sierra Nevada Mountains, he and wife Elsie settled in Laguna in 1917. Edgar was a natural leader and shortly inspired the first gallery exhibit that led to the Laguna Beach Art Association and all that followed. It was Payne who brought George Hurrell, the artist who became Hollywood's glamour photographer. Elsie Palmer Payne (1884-1971), wife to Edgar, was a noted artist in her own right. Reared in San Francisco, she studied at the Chicago Fine Arts Academy, started the Elsie Palmer Payne Art School of Laguna in 1934, and in retrospect is counted with the great Early California artists.

Norman St. Clair (1863-1912), born in England and trained in architecture, came to America and eventually settled in Pasadena. His interest turned to painting and he was the first noted artist to paint in Laguna Beach, about 1900. He exhibited his watercolors in San Francisco, where he had worked, in 1903. The show triggered a wave of interest in Laguna by painters, especially after the 1906 earthquake. St. Clair resided in Pasadena but painted frequently in Laguna, bringing artists such as Granville Redmond. St. Clair died at 48 of tuberculosis; the *N.Y. Times* carried his obituary.

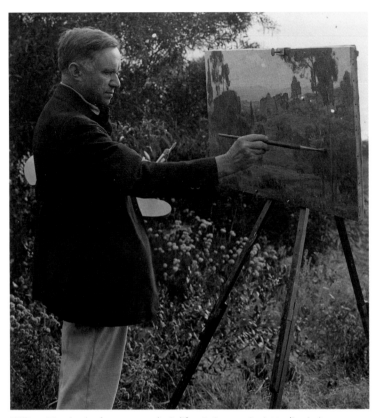

William Wendt, the foremost early California Impressionist to live in Laguna.
Credit: First American, courtesy of the Laguna Beach Historical Society.

William Wendt (1865-1946), German born, was largely self-taught
but earned the title "dean of southern California landscape painters."
Wendt's landscapes evinced a profound reverence for Nature. Because
of his prestige, he was the primary influence for the Laguna art colony.
His companions on painting expeditions into the countryside included
George Gardner Symons, Hanson Puthuff, and Edgar Payne.

Wendt married the sculptress Julia Bracken. The Wendts built a
Laguna home with studio in 1912 though they maintained their Los
Angeles studio-home, which they bought from artists Elmer and
Marion Wachtel. William came here frequently, especially during WWI
(he had a German accent, perhaps a factor) though his work was pri-
marily landscapes, not seascapes.

(Primary source: *Artists in California, 1786-1940, Volume II*, 1989,
by Edan M. Hughes.)

CHAPTER 16

Gallery Walks

Peter Blake brought modern and contemporary art to Laguna in 1993. *Photo: April Hellewell Dickson*

Mankind's search for new forms of beauty is wonderfully displayed in Laguna's many art galleries. They're open year around, staffed by art lovers willing to explain their passion, and there's no admission charge. You could call this Art 201; it's the best entertainment bargain in town. The galleries are grouped by location: North, South, and Central. This chapter covers the North and South galleries. The central galleries, scattered around downtown, are covered in the Chapter 4 walking tour. Pacific Edge stands alone at 540 S. Coast Hwy, suite 210 and is worth the walk—check the work of Bryan Mark Taylor. There are also galleries and studios in Laguna Canyon.

NOTE: If you're in town on the first Thursday of a month, be sure to check out the Art Walk, from 6:00-9:00 p.m. More a moveable party, the Art Walk is a gallery tour with music, refreshments, and entertainment plus free transportation by Laguna Beach trams.

How to visit an art gallery: In the past, being both cheap and naïve of art, I didn't know how to talk to gallery staff so their expertise was wasted. On recent visits I explained how I was writing a book for the more thoughtful and curious Laguna visitor and wanted to include their gallery. They were most helpful (and provided the basis for my observations below).

So start your visit with a question in mind. If you don't have a query, try one like this: *I'm not an expert, yet, but want to add art in my home; could you suggest how to get started?* You can't lose with this question. The typical gallery carries art in a range of prices, from a few hundred dollars to tens of thousands. The big buyers feed them today but their future lies in the new buyer, so even a novice gets respect. They may introduce you to younger artists who don't yet command the big bucks but whose work should grow in value. So ask questions, get acquainted with the galleries, and find something you like to start your collection. No other purchase gives the lasting pleasure of art.

Jeff Wood of Len Wood's Indian Territory Gallery with Maria pottery. *Photo: April Hellewell Dickson.*

THE NORTH GALLERIES (300 block of N. Coast Hwy.)

Getting started: Start at the Laguna Museum of Art, between Heisler Park and Main Beach, 307 Cliff Drive. Walk across the street to Len Wood's Indian Territory.

💜 **Len Wood's Indian Territory**, 305 N. Coast: Start your walk with Indian art—they lived here for over 99% of our history and Indian Territory, more a museum that a gallery, has a fabulous collection of ceramics, jewelry, blankets, and other Indian art. I rank this as one of our top five galleries; don't miss it. Posted hours are 11-4, Tue-Sat, but if they're not there email "info@indianterritory.com" to make an appointment.

Directions: Cross the street (be safe, use the crosswalk).

JoAnne Artman Gallery, 326 N. Coast: Presents a variety of award-winning contemporary artists.

💜 **Sue Greenwood Fine Art**, 330 N. Coast, features established contemporary West Coast artists. The term *Narrative Realism* was used, which I gathered means art that tells a true story. You can learn a lot in an art gallery.

Mark Timothy Gallery, 350 N Coast: offers fine art photographs and guest contemporary work.

Adam Neeley Fine Art Jewelry, 352 N. Coast: Neeley make jewelry that's also art.

Kelsey Michaels Fine Art, 354 N. Coast, is an artist/art dealer family business offering contemporary and mixed-media art.

Nicholson's Antiques, 362 N. Coast: Since '73, a good place if you live at the intersection of art and antiques.

💜 **Lu Martin Galleries**, 372 N. Coast: Here since '88, Lu's collection includes seascapes by Alfredo Gomez, Zen paintings by Martin Beaupre, abstracts by Greg Martin, & scenes by Brooke Harker.

Quorum Art Gallery, 374 N. Coast: A unique gallery for two reasons—first, it's a coop, meaning a small group of twelve artists operate the gallery so you talk to real artists, and second, among art galleries this is a real survivor, here since 1963. The artists come and go, but the institution lives on. Mostly *plein air* work in a variety of styles.

Laguna North Gallery, 376 N. Coast: Another coop gallery, which means you'll see a variety of styles by great local artists.

Studio 7 Gallery, 384B N. Coast: This is also a co-op, featuring Impressionist oil work by excellent artists, much of it *plein air.*

Sandstone Gallery, 384A N. Coast: At the same site since 1981, this charming co-op gallery has excellent artists creating contemporary fine art.

El Paseo is a collection of small galleries and shops built around a patio at 414-22 N. Coast.

THE SOUTH GALLERIES (1400 & 1500 blocks, S. Coast Hwy.) This historic art district with its landmark '30s cottages is part of the HIP District, named for its 'historic and interesting places.'

Selanne Steak Tavern, 1464 S. Coast, this landmark 1934 cottage, later the popular French 75 restaurant, is now associated with Teemu Selanne, the hockey star known as the Finnish Flash, whose number was recently retired by the Anaheim Ducks. Visit the South Galleries in the afternoon and make this your dinner stop.

The Art Center, 1492 S. Coast: Art galleries have clustered here since 1942. **Cove Gallery**, an original in Laguna since 1973, is artist-owned with a variety of quality work. **Water Color Gallery**, owned by the charming Lucille McElroy, has offered watercolors by local and international artists for 25 years. **Salt Fine Art** includes interesting work by Latin American artists.

Bluebird Gallery, 1540 S. Coast, has offered excellent contemporary California art since 1978.

♥ **The Redfern Gallery**, 1540 S. Coast, has the best collection of Early California Impressionists, including original Laguna artists Edgar Payne, William Wendt, Granville Redmond and Joseph Kleitsch. One of the top five galleries in my view; don't miss it.

Vladimir Sokolov Gallery, 1540 S. Coast, in Laguna since 1980, presents unique works by Vladimir Sokolov, a "mixture of acrylic, paper, and music."

♥ **DeRu's Fine Arts**, in the Bluebird Center at 1590 S. Coast, has an exceptional collection of Early California Impressionists rivaled only by The Redfern Gallery (see above). Owner Dewitt McCall also offers museum-quality art restoration.

Roberta Haltom, Director of The Redfern Gallery. *Photo: April Hellewell Dickson.*

We hope you enjoyed your gallery tour. Offering art to the public is a fickle business; you've likely noticed that just a few galleries have survived more than a decade. Give them your support; they've helped continue Laguna's tradition as an art colony.

THE BEACHES

As much as anything, it's the waves that draw people to Laguna. Children play in them, artists paint them, surfers ride them, and youthful girls of all ages sunbath besides them. Would surfing have ever taken off without those girls watching?

The restless, repeating rhythm of the waves stirs something within us all. Children, in spite of their limited attention span, never tire of the beach. And there's something to that saying, you know, that if you're lucky enough to live by the beach, well then, you're lucky enough.

ABOVE: Sunset at Three Arch Bay. *Photo: David Laws*

But the beauty of the beaches is available to all. Laguna, graced by seven miles of coastline divided by bays and coves, offers several dozen beaches. Chapter 17 talks about the beaches in more detail, but you can have a great afternoon at any beach—the magical elements of sand, sunshine, and waves are everywhere.

Some beaches are uniquely good for surfing, diving, or paddling—we'll talk about things you can do in Chapter 18. Laguna Beach played a central role in the rise of the surfing culture so we'll briefly recount the history of wave riding in Chapter 19.

CHAPTER 17

The Beaches of Laguna

Laguna has seven miles of coastline; the most visited beaches are in central Laguna, around Heisler Park, Main Beach, and the street beaches from Sleepy Hollow to Bluebird Canyon. Crystal Cove State Park, with 3.5 miles of beach, is to the north of the city. Aliso Beach, managed by the county, is in south Laguna. Further south, past the city limits, is Monarch Beach and adjoining Salt Creek Beach, the latter a county park with parking.

Below is a brief summary of Laguna's public beaches. Warning: Respect the ocean; it's beautiful to look at but it can be deadly. Visitors should only use beaches with lifeguards on duty; when you arrive, check the color of the flag flying and ask the lifeguard about safety issues.

The Laguna Beach Department of Marine Safety has an excellent website providing information about beaches and links to surf reports, tide tables, marine forecasts, and water quality reports. Visit the website at: www.lagunabeachcity.net/cityhall/marine/.

The map on page 64 lists 24 of Laguna's beaches. Here we comment on the more notable beaches.

Heisler Park provides a scenic bluff top walk but also offers a string of beaches (for more see Chapter 1).

Main Beach is a three-ring circus complete with basketball and volleyball courts, a table for chess or checkers (a work of public art), a boardwalk, and a playground for children. (For more see Chapter 2.)

THE BEACHES OF
LAGUNA BEACH

NEWPORT BEACH ↑

Crystal Cove State Park

Irvine Cove

Emerald Bay

Pacific Coast Highway

Crescent Bay
Shaw's Cove
Fisherman's Cove
Diver's Cove
Rockpile

Broadway/Laguna Canyon

Main Beach
Sleepy Hollow

Legion St.

Cleo St Beach
St. Ann's St Beach
Thalia St Beach
Oak St Beach
Brooks St Beach
Cress St Beach
Mountain St Beach
Bluebird St Beach
Agate St Beach
Pearl St Beach

Thalia St.

Brooks St.

Bluebird Canyon

Wood's Cove

Moss Point

Victoria Beach

Nyes Place

Treasure Island

Aliso Beach

Camel Point Beach

West St. Beach

Table Rock Beach

1000 Steps

West St.

Three Arch Bay

MONARCH BEACH ↓

The Street Beaches run from Sleepy Hollow to Bluebird Canyon and are named for the streets that intersect Coast Hwy (see map). If you grew up in Village Laguna (the older area between Broadway and Bluebird Canyon) you likely identify with the beach closest to your street. There's a strong sense of loyalty to one's beach, even though to a visitor the beaches may look similar. Surfers are welcome at Pearl, Brook's, Thalia, St. Anne's and Rockpile at Heisler Park.

The Brooks Street Surf Classic is 50 years old, making it the world's oldest surfing contest. There's no certain date—the start of a waiting period is announced and the contest happens whenever the surf is judged good enough. There's one rule however: you must be a local.

Moss Point is worth a visit just for the landmark homes (see Chapter 11), but nearby is Wood's Cove, a famous subject of post-WWII artist, Robert W. Wood, also well known for its "blowhole." Ruby Street Park, though small and lacking beach access, is a delightful place to enjoy lunch by the sea.

Victoria Beach doesn't have the best parking (you may have to walk a bit), but is Laguna's best skimboarding beach. It also has the novelty of what looks like a lighthouse against the cliff that once was a private staircase to the beach built in 1936. Public access is by the staircase near the corner of Victoria and Sunset; be careful parking, some of the streets are private.

Aliso Creek Beach is mostly a visitor's beach but does have the advantage of parking on the beach, or across the street. The waves tend to be shorebreaks and in storms can be pounders, so care is needed. Check with the lifeguard.

Aliso Beach is bordered by two unique homes with spectacular ocean views. To the north beyond Aliso Creek is the "Rock House," a contemporary mansion that appears to be build into the rocky earth but presides over the beach. Perched on the bluff to the south is "Villa Gucci," a French Riviera-style mansion built on property once owned by Charlie Chaplin (they torn down the home but his gazebo survives).

South Laguna Beaches stretching from Aliso Creek Beach southward are a series of beaches accessed from Coast Hwy. on the bluff (meaning lots of steps). The beaches in order are Camel Point, West St. (not identified by a sign; a popular gay beach), Table Rock (small but perhaps Laguna's prettiest), and at 9th Avenue, 1000 Steps (actually 218 steps but still a good workout). Thousand Steps is popular with locals, though you must find parking on adjacent streets. At the south end, accessible at low tides, is a remarkable cave.

4

CHAPTER 18

Things to Do

Paddleboarding has been around for a while; back in the day rentals were just 25 cents an hour. *Credit: Photo from Susan Adcock Osbom Photograph Collection, courtesy of the Laguna Beach Historical Society.*

Laguna can be as good for your body as for your soul.

If you want to be active, there are a remarkable variety of choices. Main Beach is one of the beaches with sand volleyball courts (site of the world's 2nd oldest men's open tournament held each June; there's also a women's open in May) as well as basketball courts. You can ride the waves as a surfer or skimboarder, paddle a kayak or stand up paddleboard, or just swim in the ocean, if you're a good swimmer. You can explore underwater as a scuba diver or snorkeler; some claim Laguna's reefs and kelp forests offer the best diving on the southern California coast.

You can hike or mountain bike the 22,000 acres of the Laguna Greenbelt (see Chapter 34), or try street riding in the historic neighborhoods (see chapters 9, 10 and 11, though I'd avoid busy Coast Highway). And if you're a runner, you can go wherever the bikes go, plus you have the beauty of the surfline along the beaches. There are also tennis courts, at the high school and behind the Festival of Arts grounds. At The Ranch—a Laguna icon re-envisioned as a coastal ranch resort—Ben Brown's Golf Course offers a relaxed game of golf on a 9-hole course carved out of historic Thurston Ranch. (Call 800 223 3309) Yes, Laguna can be as good for your body as for your soul.

The picturesque coves of Laguna that drew the artists a century ago now offer a new, fast-growing attraction: stand-up paddleboarding (SUP). It's a great way to experience the ocean and appreciate the beauty of the coast. Paddleboarding services became so popular the city enacted ordinances enforced by Marine Safety that require a certified teacher for every four paddlers and a limit of ten per group. You can also rent paddleboards but for the visitor or uninitiated starting in a class is safer and you'll learn more. (Besides the stores noted below, you can get your SUP start with Erin O'Malley's Sunset Paddle, 949/939-3114; Goff Stepien's Goff Tours, 949/715 4120; and Sealegs, 1444 S. Coast, 949/715 9098.)

Below is a list of shops that might help you enjoy Nature in Laguna—after many years I was unaware of some of these services so include them as research for visitors. We even included The Guitar Shoppe, a Laguna icon, if you want to exercise your fingers with a little picking.

Shops at Thalia St. (900 block) and Coast Hwy:

Second Reef Surf Shop (903 S. Coast Hwy; 949/715 7732) is a Billabong store. They offer rental boards and surfing lessons.

Thalia Surf Shop (915 S. Coast Hwy; 949/497 3292) rents (soft) surf-boards and wetsuits. Lessons are taught at nearby Thalia St. Beach; call a day in advance to catch the best waves.

Shops at Oak St. (1100 block) and Coast Hwy:

Rip Curl (1099 S. Coast Hwy; 949/715 4885) is one of the Rip Curl owned stores, a small, private company that has stayed close to its surfing roots. They offer new and rental boards, wetsuits, beach apparel and accessories.

Laguna Surf and Sport (1088 S. Coast Hwy; 949/497 7000) has outfit-ted surfers since 1982 (originally Oak St. Surf Shop, now owned by Volcom of France). They rent (soft) surfboards and teach at Thalia; call a day in advance to schedule for the best waves. Boogie boards are available to rent.

Handplant Skate Shop (1025 S. Coast Hwy; 949/715 4070) offers equipment and accessories for skateboarders.

Brawner Boards (1103 S. Coast Hwy; 949/480 7649) offers SUP and surfboards, beach apparel, and lessons. Lessons are taught at nearby Oak St. Beach; with an hour of notice they can usually get you going.

La Vida Laguna (1257 S. Coast Hwy; 949/275 7544) serves Laguna with two stores—this one by the surfing beaches, the other (see next page) near Boat Canyon. They rent surfboards and provide lessons plus other services.

A seagull and a surfer, barely visible in the morning mist, checking the waves.
Photo: David Laws

Shops in the Boat Canyon Area:

La Vida Laguna (673 N. Coast Hwy, one of two sites; 949/275 7544) offers the greatest variety of activities, including daily kayak tours (9:00 and 11:00 a.m.), stand up paddleboard lessons and equipment, and photo hikes for photographers.

Laguna Sea Sports (925 N. Coast Hwy; 949/494 6955) is located just above Shaw's Cove, a favorite of scuba divers. Laguna is famous for its dive spots and Laguna Sea Sports has served divers for decades. If you're a diver you know about them; if diving is on your "bucket list," Laguna Sea Sports will get you started.

Other Laguna Beach Shops:

Hobie Sports (294 Forest Ave; 949/497 3304) carries products of Hobie Alder, the local kid (his folks had a summer home above Oak St. Beach) who became a legendary surfing innovator and businessman. No one has defined modern surfing more than Hobie. The store offers surfing gear, lots of apparel, and rents boogie boards. They don't provide surfing lessons in the Laguna store.

Victoria Skimboards (2955 Laguna Canyon Rd, about 2 miles from Coast Hwy; phone 949/494 0059), founded 1976, is the leading skimboard maker. Founder Tex Haines, a skimboard legend, now solely owns Victoria. The history of skimboards can be seen on the walls. Victoria rent skimboards, provide lessons, and runs a summer camp for kids age 7 and up.

Laguna Cyclery (240 Thalia St; 949/494 1522) is a full service cycling shop. They offer rentals of both road or mountain bikes and are a storehouse of biking information. Laguna is home to Swiss-born mountain biking legend Hans "No Way" Rey—does that inspire you to try our wilderness trails?

Costa Azul (689 S. Coast; 949/497 1423) is the surf shop of Rod Greenup, a Laguna Beach original since '91. If you want to try surfing or stand up paddling Rod might rent you some equipment and teach you the basics.

Soul Surf (763 S. Coast Hwy; 949/6370463), a surfing school offering private and group lessons, surf camps, etc.

The Guitar Shoppe (1027 N. Coast Hwy; 949/497 2110) is a Laguna icon for guitar players. They sell guitars, teach, and hand-build custom instruments. Kirk Sand, a guitar builder since the '70s, builds for "finger style" players including professionals ranging from Chet Atkins to Jose Feliciano. If you're into guitars, check out The Guitar Shoppe.

4

CHAPTER 19

A Brief History of Wave Riding

Duke Kahanamoku, 1920 *Credit: Uncredited staff photographer, Los Angeles Times, courtesy of Fotor.com*

Surfing was practiced anciently by Pacific Islanders, first documented on Captain Cook's 1778 voyage: ". . . they seem to feel a great pleasure in the motion which this Exercise gives." Surfing was discouraged in Hawaii's missionary era, but was still practiced when author Jack London visited in 1907. London was taken with the beauty of surfing, writing of one surfer, "I saw him tearing in on the back of [a wave] standing upright with his board, carelessly poised, a young god bronzed with sunburn." London understood surfing.

That "young god" was George Freeth, born of an Irish father in Oahu, who later introduced surfing to California. Freeth was followed by Duke Kahanamoku (shown in photo with longboard), the fastest swimmer of his time, who demonstrated surfing at Corona del Mar on his way to the 1912 Olympics. The Duke was more than a surfer who could swim fast; he is also remembered as the "Ambassador of Aloha." Kahanamoku introduced the Hawaiian way of peacefulness towards mankind and Nature—the "spirit of aloha"—which is the surfing community's contribution to Laguna's uniqueness.

TWO LAGUNA INNOVATORS

Hobie Alter (1933-2014): The heavy wooden *longboards* traditionally used in Hawaii were more suited to the giant surf there than the waves of California. An innovator was needed. Down in Laguna Beach, during the summer of 1950, teenager Hobart "Hobie" Alter started shaping surfboards in his father's garage near Oak Street beach. First he built balsa longboards (9 to 10 feet long) and opened a store in Dana Point to sell his boards. In 1958 Hobie teamed up with Gordon "Grubby" Clark to built lighter, shorter (5-6 ft.) boards of foam they coated with fiberglass. Starting in Laguna Canyon—the Silicon Valley of the surf industry—they revolutionized the sport by providing short, buoyant boards suited to the Southern California surf.

Hobie would have starved shaping boards for the few surfers of the time without Hollywood. The 1959 movie *Gidget* jump-started a cultural revolution built around the beach. Fuel was added to the fire by Beach Boys' songs, like *Summer Days*, and *Good Vibrations*. But even before the Beach Boys, guitar player Dick Dale was lighting up screaming fans at the Balboa Rendezvous Ballroom with the heavy beat of surf classics like *Pipeline*. It helped that Leo Fender up in Fullerton was building ever more powerful amplifiers and speakers.

All this made surfers the coolest guys around and millionaires out of surf-businessmen like Hobie Alter. It also packed the beaches—and highways—of Laguna. Popularity isn't always a good thing but somehow surfing escaped the decadence of Hollywood, drawn more to the example of Duke Kahanamoku and the *spirit of aloha*. So if you're in the surf store and the clerk wishes you well by saying, "no worries,"— that's *aloha*, another of the spiritual roots that make Laguna Beach unique. And this is a brief history of surfing in 500 words.

(Sources include From Polynesia, *With Love; The History of Surfing From Captain Cook to the Present*, by Ben Marcus, posted at surfingforlife.com.)

This Victoria Beach photo catches exuberant skimboarders in all the phases of their sport. *Photo: Unknown photographer, courtesy of Victoria Skimboards.*

Tex Haines: Skimboarding is a uniquely Laguna sport, started by Main Beach lifeguards using plywood disks back in the '20s. Innovation occurred here also: high-tech skimboards, shaped like surfboards but flatter and without the skeg, have replaced plywood. Skimboarding is newer and still a microsport but its popularity is spreading. The most prestigious competition is the Victoria World Skimboarding Championship, held here at Aliso Creek Beach. Victoria Skimboards, founded in Laguna Canyon back in 1976 is the dominant manufacturer, now solely owned by founder Charles "Tex" Haines, a skimboard legend.

Haines's family rented a summer cottage at Victoria Beach when he was a kid, and his summers evolved into a pattern of either surfing San Onofre, or skimboarding at Victoria. He graduated from Stanford with the idea of becoming a veterinarian, but wound up working at Rainbow Sandals back in the day, and that evolved into building skimboards with childhood friend Peter Prietto, and founding Victoria Skimboards. Despite his achievements Haines is modest and approachable, crediting his success to his wife, or to his parents who taught him the simple precepts of doing the right thing, just being fair, and enjoying life. He lives the aloha spirit taught by Duke Kahanamoku, and tells of getting goose pimples when he met the Duke (and still gets them when he speaks of it). Haines exemplifies the true *waterman*—one who finds peace and harmony in the ocean, and carries it with him on land.

Riding skimboards is spectator friendly due to closeness—the best beaches have waves breaking close to shore. The rider starts on the beach and run towards a developing wave, throwing the board down on the wet sand, stepping onto it, gliding into and then working the incoming wave, much like a surfer. The flatter beaches like Victoria Beach are a good place to get started; beaches like Aliso Creek Beach with strong shorebreaks are for the more experienced.

This is a good sport for kids not big enough to surf, or for anyone who likes to run and won't get hurt crashing into a wave. If you want a teacher to help get started, contact Victoria Skimboards (2955 Laguna Canyon Road, 949/494 0059, email info@victoriaskimboards. com). Victoria rents skimboards for a reasonable price and has a summer camp for kids.

"The highest art is the art of living," William E Brown counseled in a 1935 speech cited by *OC Weekly*. Judging by the romantic *Pirate's Tower*, a Victoria Beach stairway to their 1926 Tudor-French Provincial home on the bluff, the Brown family definitely knew how to live. The home, known as La Tour (2683 Victoria Drive), was later a residence of actress Bette Davis. The building behind the tower is Villa Rockledge. *Photo: David Laws*

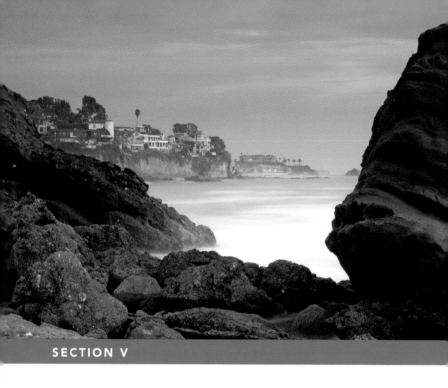

LAGUNA CHARACTERS

Only a wide variety of characters could create a town so unique as Laguna, but most who settled here were practical, provident, hard-working family people. But this is a town that has welcomed troubled folks too. When you drive down the canyon to Main Beach, you've hit the end of the road—you can't get any further from whatever you're leaving behind without getting wet. Over the years many a burdened soul has stopped here and for most it has been a place of healing. Laguna has been home to some truly outrageous and unconventional folks, to whom we dedicate this section. Here we present a few, in order of their arrival.

Photo: David Laws

Pancho Barnes (1901-1975) was born into money but didn't fit the mold of the typical debutante. So she took up flying, a man's business in those days, and made a name for herself at the dawn of the aviation age. Eliler Larsen (1890-1975) was the WWI version of Forest Gump. Like Gump he criss-crossed the country on foot until he discovered Laguna Beach, a place that would accept him and his "mission of friendliness." Richard Halliburton (1900-1939), adventurer, writer, and lecturer, was perhaps the best-known man of his time. He died in his most outrageous adventure and was soon forgotten. In Laguna we remember him for the unusual home he left behind. Hollywood in Laguna started with the silent film stars and continues to this day.

CHAPTER 20
Pancho Barnes

Tom Wolfe wrote a classic bestseller about the space program called, *The Right Stuff*. The book told of test pilots like Chuck Yeager, combat veterans of WWII and Korea, who did the dangerous work of testing new jets out in the desert at Edwards Air Force Base. In the evenings they could relax at the Happy Bottom Riding Club, a dude ranch bar run by a fiftyish, overweight and rather masculine woman nick-named Pancho Barnes. The remarkable thing is the affection those hot test pilots had for Pancho. Chuck Yeager remembers: "Pancho was a different kind of woman, tough as nails. She knew a lot about flying." So who was Pancho Barnes? The short version is that Florence Lowe "Pancho" Barnes (1901-1975) grew up in a wealthy San Marino family with a 40-acre summer estate overlooking Crescent Bay in Laguna Beach. Pancho wasn't a pretty girl, a bit husky actually, and never fit the society mold. She decided she could "either apologize for who I was or bust out and do whatever I want." Flying, it turned out, was what Pancho wanted. Flying became Pancho's life mission; she ran a barnstorming show, competed in early air races for women, broke Amelia Earhart's women's speed record, and flew in movies as a stunt pilot. Laguna Beach was a better fit for Pancho than San Marino so she built a runway at her Laguna estate, about where McKnight Drive is now, Laguna's first and only airfield.

Pancho argued that when you had a choice in life, you might as well choose "happy." She flew fast and partied hard, but the Depression happened and one day the music stopped—Pancho had run out of

Pancho always said, "When you have a choice in life, choose 'happy'."
Credit: From the Archives of the International Women's Air & Space Museum, photographer unknown.

money. Undeterred she bought some cheap land out in the desert and started over, farming alfalfa and building a dude ranch with a landing strip. By good fortune, the adjacent dry lake became Edwards AFB and the rest is history. Now, years later, the test pilots return once a year for "Pancho Barnes Day" to keep her memory alive. By reading this story, so are you.

(Sources: the documentary, The Legend of Pancho Barnes and the Happy Bottom Riding Club, and the biography, A Woman Called "Pancho"; Remembering Florence "Pancho" Barnes, by Nick T. Spark.)

CHAPTER 21

The Greeter

Eiler Larsen was a Danish immigrant who dedicated his life to greeting perfect strangers. He called this unusual habit his "mission of friendliness." You may have noticed that Laguna is an unusually friendly town. Being friendly is deep in the town's DNA. So consider this: Could one eccentric man change the culture of a town simply by being friendly? I have started to believe this could be true, which forces me to include his story in our study of Laguna's spiritual roots.

Larsen was the WWI version of Forest Gump. He fought in that war, returned to the U.S. and hiked the 2200 miles of the Appalachian Trail, and then turned westward in his journey. He marched to a different drummer, you know, and I suspect he was run out of any number of towns along the way. Though a simple person, he was a little too different for most folks to tolerate. Had they met, the fictional Forest Gump would have understood Eiler Larsen.

Larsen was in northern California when artist friends thought he might like Laguna Beach. So Larsen came to visit and concluded his friends were right: Laguna was the perfect place for his "mission of friendliness." Eiler's true joy was to stand at the corner of Forest and Coast Highway and greet perfect strangers, whether afoot or in their car, with a booming "H-e-l-l-o, how are you." This wasn't any youthful folly; Larsen was 52 when he settled here in 1942.

He worked a little as a gardener, but just enough to get by. After work he would hurry to what he called "the office," the corner where he greeted the ever-passing stream of humanity. Before Laguna he had lived for a time in San Francisco; there he was intrigued to hear of our Pageant of the Masters. For three years, before moving to Laguna, he came for the Pageant and played the role of Judas in the final scene, *The Last Supper*.

After his passing a statute was erected to Larsen near his "office," at Coast Highway and Forest. Larsen also worked a little at the old Pottery Shack, and a statue remembers him there also. Larsen was incapable of greed. He had nothing and desired nothing. This wasn't through ignorance; Larsen spoke six languages and was a voracious reader. But all the books he acquired were given away, often to the Laguna library. For this reason, the short street behind the library is named Eiler Larsen Lane.

Once, in the off-season, Eiler took his mission to Palm Springs. The townspeople, not appreciating his friendly spirit, complained. So the

Eiler Larsen, the official Laguna Beach greeter. *Photo: From the Thomas Pulley Postcard Collection, courtesy of the Laguna Beach Historical Society.*

police chased Eiler away and he walked back to Laguna. Later, reflecting on his life, Larsen observed: "Some people have millions of dollars and no friends. I've got practically nothing and thousands of friends drive by to greet me." Larsen lived his life differently—he marched to drums others couldn't hear. But through his mission of friendliness he lived a beautiful life and, I believe, changed the culture of a town. *(Sources include Wikipedia.)*

CHAPTER 22

Richard Halliburton

Richard Halliburton (1900-1939), in the '20s and '30s, was the world's best-known adventurer. Then he died during his most outrageous expedition and was forgotten. The method for Halliburton's fame was to visit famous places around the world, break whatever rules hindered him, and then lecture and write about his adventure. Halliburton avoided convention and sought publicity in what he termed his chase for "distant horizons." A 1925 book, *The Royal Road to Romance*, was dedicated to his Princeton roommates, whose "sanity, consistency, and respectability . . . drove me to this book."

Halliburton made Laguna his home in the '30s, building the iconic "Hangover House" on Ceanothus Street. The cubic concrete building was named either for its precarious perch over a 500-foot bluff offering incredible views, or for Halliburton's parties. Regardless, it's a remarkable part of Laguna's architectural history though Halliburton only lived there briefly before starting his next—and final—adventure.

There was one problem: To stay in the spotlight each adventure had to be more outrageous than the last. He retraced Cortez's invasion and conquest of Mexico; climbed mountains, including the Matterhorn, Popocatepetl, and Mt. Fuji; swam the Hellespont in imitation of English poet Lord Byron Strait, as well as the Panama Canal registered as a ship (paying 36 cents passage based on his weight); repeated Hannibal's crossing of the Alps (using a rented Paris zoo elephant); and flew around the world in an open-cockpit biplane (with the capable Moye Stephens as pilot; they crossed oceans by ship).

His last feat was to cross the Pacific Ocean in a traditional Chinese junk and sail into San Francisco Bay for the 1939 Golden Gate International Exposition. It seemed a great idea so Halliburton and friends traveled to China, had a junk named the *Sea Dragon* built, and sailed for the U.S. It was an ill-fated adventure and the junk disappeared with all hands in a mid-Pacific typhoon. As the storm grew a cheerful message sent from the *Sea Dragon* said, "Having a wonderful time. Wish you were here instead of me." The only possible remain of the ship ever found was a rudder washed ashore on a California beach in 1945.

(Sources: The Royal Road to Adventure, R. Halliburton, 1925; Wikipedia.)

CHAPTER 23

Hollywood in Laguna

Moving pictures were the technical marvel of the early 1900s. The noted silent film director D. W. Griffith made the first Hollywood movie, titled *In Old California*. In 1915 he directed and produced the (possibly) most profitable movie of all time, *The Birth of a Nation*, acclaimed for innovative technique but decried for the glorification of the Ku Klux Klan. (In his defense, Griffith's father had been a colonel in the Confederate Army).

In 1919 a group of leading Hollywood figures, wishing to circumvent the monopolistic *studio system*, formed *United Artists*. The founders— D. W. Griffith, Mary Pickford, Douglas Fairbanks, Charlie Chaplin, and William G. McAdoo, a politically connected lawyer and President Woodrow Wilson's Treasury Secretary—visited or had homes in Laguna Beach. Pickford and Fairbanks starred at the opening of Pacific Coast Highway in 1926 and the South Coast Theatre in 1933.

Charlie Chaplin had a home on the bluff over Aliso Beach, it's said, where the Gucci home now stands at 1 Camel Point. Slim Summerville, a comedian who appeared in several Chaplin films, made Laguna his home, living on the beach in Sleepy Hollow. His residence, later the Beach House restaurant, is now the Driftwood Kitchen (see Chapter 24).

In 1927 *The Jazz Singer* with Al Jolson—the first movie with synchronized sound—made silent movies obsolete and studios had to restock their inventory. It was a blessing to Laguna as it catered to movie filming during the Great Depression. As a child I recall watching the 1934 remake of Robert Louis Stevenson's classic, *Treasure Island*. Goff Island, named for an early Laguna homesteader, acquired a new name from the movie filmed there.

Bette Davis (1908-1989), one of the great cinema actresses with ten Oscar nominations, lived many years in Laguna. Davis had a great career, playing tough roles and gaining ten Oscar nominations. The famous cigarette scene in *Now, Voyager* was filmed on the patio of Victor Hugo's restaurant, now Las Brisas. Her movie *A Stolen Life* with Glenn Ford was filmed at Treasure Island. There is a local story, from the old Dilley's Bookstore. Bette, at the height of her fame, picked out a stack of books and airily told the owner, Jim Dilley, to put it on her account. Dilley, a Laguna character (see Chapter 33), responded with a straight face, "Yes Madam, and what is the name?"

Stars still hang out in Laguna. Keep your eyes open—you may have a sighting.

Photo: David Laws

RESTAURANTS

Laguna is of necessity a restaurant town—the many visitors need to eat. The unique thing about our restaurants is most are locally owned and that's a good thing.

The big change in recent years is the rooftop lounge. It started at the old La Casa del Camino hotel, was a big hit, expanded to Mozambique, and now to the Skyloft, just opened by Mozambique's owner. The restaurant business is tough. Since the 1st Edition of *Loving Laguna* in early 2013, eight restaurants have died. So though prices are higher close to the beach, trust that everyone's working hard to give you the best dining experience for your money. In the food business, survival is part of the art. In this section we give you a bird's eye view of Laguna's food offering organized by:

- Breakfast places (they also offer lunch and a few dinner),
- Casual food (bakeries, dairy foods, hamburgers, pizza, and tacos),
- Dinner (sorted by American, French, Italian, Mexican, and Asian),
- Special occasion dining, for that forget-the-cost celebration.

If you wish to dig deeper try Diane Armitage's book, *The Best of Laguna Beach*. 'Bon appétit', or if you're eating Latin, 'buen provecho'.

♥ = Editor's pick

CHAPTER 24

Breakfast by the Beach

Photo: David Laws

You can't beat Laguna for breakfast spots. The ocean is essential to the perfect Laguna breakfast: The morning sun lights the salty foam, the sea smell delights the senses, and the seagulls shriek their approval. When you walk away from breakfast comfortably full and feel the warm sun on your back, you've given the day a darn good start.

BREAKFAST BY THE SEA: Here are Laguna's best beach breakfasts, presented from north to south. All serve lunch; a few offer dinner.

Madison Square, 320 N. Coast, is a gift shop inside and a breakfast-lunch place outside in the gardens; you order at the counter.

Urth Caffé, 308 N. Coast, this is the newest and hottest place for organic coffee and fine tea—just remember you're also paying for the remodel of a historic home. There's a chef on duty, they say, so the food should improve.

Las Brisas, 361 Cliff Drive is on the bluff above Main Beach and offers a buffet style all-you-can-eat brunch with made-to-order omelets. It's not as personal as other places but there's a lot of history here and the dining room is great for visiting. Try for a window seat. We bring visitors here for brunch but it's also a great place to enjoy the sunset.

Greeter's Corner, 329 S. Coast, this isn't our first choice for breakfast by the beach, but they have a great patio overlooking Main Beach.

White House Café, 340 S. Coast, said to be the oldest restaurant in Orange County. It's been on this block since 1918 and once was Laguna's nicest restaurant. Now closeness to Main Beach makes it a visitor's place but locals do come for breakfast, especially the weekend brunch. Come here to connect with history and say you've eaten at the White House.

OceanView Bar & Grill, 425 S. Coast, at historic Hotel Laguna; the terrace is right on the sand, as close as you can get to the water. Check the old photographs in the hall as you enter. There's inside dining but the beach is the attraction so dining is casual.

♥ **Nick's Laguna Beach**, 440 S. Coast, is just across from the Hotel Laguna. There isn't a lot of ocean view but it's close. Nick's is new and well run. Here we met Mark, a Silicon Valley refugee, stopping for his morning cup. He sold his Palo Alto home, he said, to live in the warmth of the sun by the sea.

Driftwood Kitchen, 619 Sleepy Hollow, practically on the beach, open all day but it's more about the Stateroom Bar, open 5-12 pm. Once the home of Slim Summerville the silent movie era actor-comedian who played a Keystone Kop.

♥ **Penguin Café**, 981 S. Coast, is a breakfast and lunch place for locals. You can't actually see the ocean here but the Penguin stays busy; it's the kind of place your grandfather enjoyed in his day.

♥ **Coyote Grill**, 31621 S. Coast; there's an ocean view from the back patio so this south Laguna hangout gets on the breakfast list. Also a popular dinner spot.

The Cliff, 577 S. Coast; people love the view, so enjoy it with breakfast or sunset drinks. And check out nearby Brown's Park.

BREAKFAST IN THE VILLAGE: You get better value without the ocean view.

Anastasia, 470 Ocean, a combination café (counter order) and boutique popular with the ladies, serving breakfast and lunch. The caramel French toast is to die for.

Zinc Café & Market, 350 Ocean, is more than breakfast with good coffee. Besides lunch there's now dinner. Laguna ladies socialize in the outdoor patio, digging the organic menu.

Orange Inn Cafe, 703 S. Coast, started back in 1931, on the Irvine Ranch alongside the new Pacific Coast Highway, when roadside stands started selling the new health drink—fresh orange juice. John Bodrero moved to this 1924 cottage in '86 and developed a local following with his smoothies, muffins, breakfast dishes, and sandwiches. It's good for lunch also.

The Stand Natural Food Restaurant, 238 Thalia, next to Laguna Cyclery, home of the Hav A Chip, has been here since the early '70s, dishing out smoothies, soups, healthy vegan food snacks, and coffee. It really is a "stand" with limited seating but a favorite with locals.

Laguna Coffee Company, 1050 S. Coast, has been serious about coffee since 1991. I've never read a customer complaint; try the apple strudel. Catch the Saturday jazz sessions, 10:30-12:00 a.m.

Heidelberg Café and Bistro, 1100 S. Coast, cozy and European, serves breakfast and lunch plus illy coffee.

Koffee Klatch, 1440 S. Coast: a cozy coffee, tea, breakfast, and lunch place amidst the art galleries of S. Coast Hwy.

♥ **BREAKFAST IN THE COUNTRY: Harvest Patio**, 31106 S. Coast (at *The Ranch* in Aliso Canyon); Enjoy breakfast (and lunch) in the serenity of Aliso Canyon.

BEST COFFEE: Coffee preferences vary, but this ranking is by Laguna Beach locals.

Ben's Pantry, 31106 S. Coast (at *The Ranch* in Aliso Canyon); Jean Paul's Goodies closed but Ben's Pantry has the coffee machine and maybe Laguna's best coffee.

Laguna Coffee Company, 1050 S. Coast, an indie micro-coffee roaster gathering beans from around the world. Claims the "hottest coffee in town."

Urth Caffé, 308 N. Coast, new to Laguna, offering organic heritage coffees on the best outdoor patio.

Orange Inn, serving surfers and locals since 1931, claims "Laguna's Best Coffee".

Coffee Pub, 384 Forest, Ste. 4, coffee and pastry with a great patio for visiting and taking in the downtown scene.

Starbucks, 180 N. Coast Hwy, and 184 S. Coast Hwy, must be mentioned when discussing coffee. We have two, practically side-by-side across from Main Beach, the former the old Diedrich's Coffee, the latter a hole-in-the-wall.

CHAPTER 25

Casual Food

If you had a good breakfast and are enjoying the town, you'll probably make it to dinner with a light meal along the way. So here are some great places to catch a snack during the day, organized by food type.

BAKERIES:

♥ **Andree's Patisserie**, 1456 S. Coast (look for the sidewalk sign) offers Laguna's best pastry, period. Don't come late. Try the almond croissant. Ron—the last local baker cooking from scratch—is usually a happy guy.

Scandia Bakery & Coffee Shop, 248 Forest Ave, into its 4th decade, will supply your sugar fix.

C'est La Vie, 373 S. Coast, is a little tired but has a popular pastry counter. There's a good ocean view from the back patio for a sunny breakfast or lunch.

South Swell Donuts, 31669 S. Coast, a family business offering Laguna's best donuts—they're good but it's our only shop.

DAIRY: Smoothies, it turns out, are the preferred drink of the surfing set—the Orange Inn and The Stand were local innovators back in the day. Around the surf district from Thalia down to Brooks you'll find: The Stand (238 Thalia); Orange Inn (703 S. Coast); Active Culture (1006 S. Coast); The Art of Juicing (1080 S. Coast, in the gym); and Project Juice (1100 S. Coast).

Chantilly, 202 Park Ave, is the best location for selling cold treats in Laguna, so the prices are higher and the service variable. But there it is, right in front of you, so what are you going to do?

♥ **Gelato Paradiso**, 448 S. Coast; locals love this hard-to-find gelato place in the back of Peppertree Lane. You'll know you're close when you smell the waffle cones. As long as you're here, check neighboring La Rue Du Chocolat, offering handmade chocolates.

Dolce Gelato, 247 Broadway, is also a favorite.

♥ **Banzai Bowl**, 1100 S. Coast, located by the surfer zone, is a family business. Banzai Bowl, a meal by itself, contains smoothie (acai-based), fruit, and granola for a healthy and filling snack. At busy times, it helps to call in your order ahead of time or be prepared to wait. Try the Maui Sunrise or the Diamond Head. (949/715-8989)

HAMBURGERS:

♥ **Husky Boy Burgers**, 802 N. Coast, selling good hamburgers since 1951; you can take your burger and a Root Beer Freeze and walk down to Diver's Cove.

Maro Wood Grill, 1915 S. Coast; Argentinian, offers fancier fare, but also what some call the best burger in town.

Johnny Rockets, 188 S. Coast, a chain place, conveniently located across from Main Beach.

Ruby's, 30622 S. Coast; another chain but across from Montage.

PIZZA:

BJ's Restaurant & Brewery, 280 S. Coast, another chain restaurant but the pizza is good and it's close to Main Beach, in case you want to eat on a bench and watch the world go by. They do get swamped in the summer, so call ahead and take your pizza to go.

Gina's Pizza, is a regional chain with two local stores: 610 N. Coast & 1100 S. Coast. They offer a tasty thick-crust pizza at a fair price, plus other Italian favorites; eat in or take out.

Pizza Lounge, 397 S. Coast, offers thin-crust gourmet pizza by the slice.

NEApolitan Pizzeria & Birreria, 31542 S. Coast, a bar with fired thin-crust pizza.

Zeytoon, 412 N. Coast, a Mediterranean deli with rooftop dining and their own style of pizza.

TACOS, ETC. (See also Mexican restaurants, Chapter 26):

♥ **La Sirena Grill**, 347 Mermaid St., is popular with locals and convenient to downtown. Its brother restaurant at 31622 S. Coast is more a bar, though same good food.

Rasta Taco, 170 Beach St., is new, street tacos with a Jamaican flare.

Taco Loco, 640 S. Coast, a hole-in-the-wall with sidewalk dining but serving great tacos.

♥ **Laguna Feast Mexican Food**, 801 Glenneyre St., sidewalk dining and great tacos just off the beaten path. Come for Taco Tuesday.

Wahoo's Fish Tacos, 1133 S. Coast, has been the Paddleboard Bar, the Sandbar, then La Paz restaurant, and finally Wahoo's, a favorite with the surfing class since 1988.

Papa's Tacos, 31622 Coast Hwy. A hole in the wall for locals.

CHAPTER 26

Dinner

Where to dine? You have a lot of choices; we group restaurants by cuisine, roughly ranking them by consensus ratings, with special occasion restaurants noted at chapter end. For reservations, most offer online service but phone numbers are given if restaurants are advised.

AMERICAN/CALIFORNIAN   Not always just steaks and spirits.

♥ **Centrál**, 361 Forest Ave, Ste 103, is the newest downtown restaurant and our favorite, specializing in coastal Peruvian food.

Broadway by Amar Santana (328 Glenneyre St; 949/715 8234): Progressive California cuisine in a cozy, relaxed environment (where Five Feet was).

Café Zoolu (860 Glenneyre; 949/494 6825): Mike and Toni run a smallish neighborhood place famous for swordfish. You'll need a reservation.

♥ **230 Forest Avenue** (the name is the address; 949/494 2545) and **Watermarc**, (448 S. Coast; 949/376 6272), are upscale restaurants created by chef Marc Cohen.

Nirvana Grille (303 Broadway; 949/497 0027), the work of a local family, is a great place to dine and enjoy conversation.

Sapphire Laguna (1200 S. Coast; 949/715 9888): Creative comfort food from around the world; dine inside or on the patio.

Lumberyard (384 Forest Ave; 949/715 3900): This restored 1927 Normandy-style building is reason enough to eat here—American cuisine with a large bar at Laguna's first lumberyard.

Maro Wood Grill (1915 S. Coast; 949/793 4040): Argentine cuisine in a cozy setting. Some come for the steak, but we love the burger.

♥ **Nick's Laguna Beach** (440 S. Coast; 949/376 8595): Excellent food (breakfast, lunch, dinner) though the bar is the central feature.

Selanne Steak Tavern (1464 S. Coast; 949/715 9881) is in the fondly remembered French 75 building, a historic Laguna home. Now it's an upscale grill and bar that fans of the Ducks will especially enjoy.

370 Common (370 Glenneyre; 949/494 8686): Once the Sorrento Grill; locals like it.

Driftwood Kitchen (619 Sleepy Hollow; 949/715 7700) and The Deck (627 Sleepy Hollow; 949/494 6700) are served by Chef Rainer Schwarz. Driftwood Kitchen (for years the Beach House) is the more upscale, featuring the Stateroom Bar. Both offer a great ocean view with good food.

The Cliff (577 S. Coast; 949/494 1956): More about the ocean than the food.

Mozambique (1740 S. Coast at Agate; 949/715 7777) is big, offering a steakhouse, bar, lounge, live entertainment, and now rooftop dining with an ocean view.

White House (340 S. Coast; 949/494 8088): Oldest in O.C; open all day; varied menu.

The renovated Heisler building (400 S. Coast) hosts two restaurants:

Tommy Bahama (949/376 6886) a bar and grill plus TB apparel on the ground floor,

Skyloft (714/585 7431), upstairs, with a new rooftop lounge offering live entertainment plus a gorgeous view. (Same owner as Mozambique; the prior House of Big Fish and Ice Cold Beer closed but reopened with new owners as Big Fish Tavern, 540 S. Coast, Ste. 200.)

FRENCH   Typically California cuisine influenced, meaning use of fresh local ingredients and "fusion" of other cooking traditions.

Studio at Montage: A 5-star experience; see Chapter 27.

Brussels Bistro (222 Forest Ave.): European; more beers than wines.

Dizz's As Is (2794 S. Coast; 949/494 5250): Founded by the Pitz family in 1977 in an old home; menu has Belgium influences; quaint place well worth the extra drive.

C'est La Vie Restaurant (373 S. Coast): Closest to Main Beach.

ITALIAN

Ristorante Rumari (1826 S. Coast; 949/494 0400): Handy to the Surf and Sand Hotel.

Romeo Cucina (249 Broadway; 949/497 6627).

Polina's Salerno (220 Beach St.): Good Italian and fair prices since '75. A favorite of locals.

Cucina Alessa (234 Forest): Convenient for shoppers.

Mare Culinary Lounge (696 S. Coast Hwy, under the Holiday Inn; 949/715 9581): Big sister to Alessa's, but with a lounge.

MEXICAN

♥ **Carmelitas** (217 Broadway; 949/715 7829): Offers Laguna's best Mexican food (and margaritas per Diane Armitage), reservation suggested. Try the crab and shrimp enchilada.

♥ **Las Brisas** (361 Cliff Dr.): Founded in 1938 as the Victor Hugo Inn, it's now part of El Torito. The view is the reason to eat here.

♥ **Coyote Grill** (31621 S. Coast): Down in south Laguna, Coyote Grill has a following among locals for casual but tasty breakfast, lunch or dinner. Features a Catalina view and daily Happy Hour.

La Sirena Grill: Sidewalk dining at 347 Mermaid, or a sports bar with food at 30862 S. Coast. Popular with locals, don't miss the Avocado Lime Salad (we like it with chicken).

Avila's Ranchito (1305 S. Coast): OK Mexican food in the historic Little Shrimp building. The basics are here—patio dining, ocean view, happy hour, taco Tuesday.

Adolfo's Mexican Food (998 S. Coast, Ste A): Not fancy but a good value.

Tortilla Republic (480 S. Coast; 949/393 4888): Inventive modern Mexican fare with a Coast Highway view.

ASIAN

♥ **Mandarin King** (1223 N. Coast, 949/494 8992): Best Chinese food in Laguna.

Tabu Grill (2892 S. Coast: 949/494 7743): Polynesian theme dinner place; highly rated by Zagat; reservations suggested.

Starfish Asian Coastal Cuisine (30832 S. Coast, across from Montage; 949/715 9200): Sister restaurant to Tabu Grill with a nightclub environment.

THAI FOOD

Thai Brothers (128 Laguna Ave.): Cozy place; pretty good Thai food; open late.

Royal Thai Cuisine (1753 S. Coast): Here for over two decades.

Laguna Thai By The Sea (31715 S. Coast): A cozy place with limited seating but take-out is an option.

6

SUSHI Lots of restaurants serve Japanese food but these five are serious about their sushi:

💜 **242 Café Fusion Sushi** (242 N. Coast) is tiny and easy to miss but for years has served up Laguna's best sushi.

San Shi Go (1100 S. Coast, Ste 303; 949/376 8786) is hidden up high in the 1100 S. coast building but their longevity attests to the quality of their sushi and Japanese food.

O Fine Japanese Cuisine (30872 S. Coast): A family-run place, near Montage.

Hapi Sushi of Laguna (250 Beach Street): Actually is a happy place.

Sushi Laguna (231 Ocean): OK sushi, OK prices.

It's A Tough Job

John Weld, former Hollywood stuntman, then local businessman, published the *Laguna Beach Post* back when Laguna was an even smaller town. He wrote a column, "Our Town," later collected into a book, *Laguna I Love You*. One story told of Francis Cabang, a Philippine immigrant who came here to make a better life, fought in WWII, worked in restaurants, and later owned a venerable institution now gone: the **Royal Hawaiian**. The Royal Hawaiian, a landmark on Coast Highway for nearly 60 years, teaches a few truisms: The American dream can work for an immigrant kid. Years of hard work are needed to build a restaurant into a community institution. And finally that the restaurant business is tough; few last for long and none last forever. The times change.

CHAPTER 27

Special Occasion Dining

BIG DEAL DINNERS: There is a time to live big and forget the cost, like the 25th anniversary of giving away your heart. Whatever, here are the options:

Studio at Montage (30801 S. Coast, in a separate building at the bluff edge; 949/715 6420): With a Forbes 5-star rating, you'll definitely need a reservation. The Studio has it all: modern French cuisine, top service, ocean view, and superior wines. This is the best you can do in Laguna.

The Loft at Montage (30801 S. Coast, in the main building; 949/715 6420): All the Montage amenities, creative American cuisine, and 150 kinds of cheese. This is the next best thing to Studio for a special event.

Splashes Restaurant (1555 S. Coast, at the Surf & Sand Resort; 949/376 2779): Great ocean view plus new executive chef Michael Reyes, formerly with Yountville's famed French Laundry.

Other extra special options: **Broadway by Amar Santana** (328 Glenneyre St; 949/715 8234); Chef Marc Cohen's **Watermarc Restaurant** (448 S. Coast; 949/376 6272) and **230 Forest Avenue** (named for its address; 949/ 494 2545); and **Sapphire Laguna** (1200 S. Coast; 949/715 9888). Live it up.

6

Photo: David Laws

THE HOMESTEADERS

Humans have hung out at Laguna Beach for a long, long time. It's a fact that the oldest human remains ever discovered in our hemisphere were found here in 1933.

Later the woman was determined to be 17,000 and perhaps 40,000 years old. Archeologists call her *Laguna Woman* and she's proof that humans have enjoyed living in Laguna for a good long time. (For more see Steve Turnbull's blogsite *light-headed.com*.)

Forty-niners settled northern California during the Gold Rush but the south remained in quiet slumber. A prolonged drought devastated the large land-grant ranchos in 1862-64, killing off cattle and causing ranches to change hands. In the Saddleback Valley, James Irvine acquired the Rancho San Joaquin and Lewis Moulton (with Basque sheepman Jean Daguerre) took over land that had been Juan Avila's Rancho Niguel. But over the adjoining coastal range, from below Aliso Creek to Laguna Creek, government-owned land—never part of a land-grant ranch—was available for homesteading. In the 1870s a group of families sharing a controversial faith claimed Laguna Beach and laid the foundation for a unique town. This is their story.

CHAPTER 28

The Thurston Family

The George and Sarah Thurston family comprised the first permanent settlers of Laguna Beach. They left the Utah Territory after the kidnapping and death of their cherubic child Rosa by Indians, traveled by railroad to San Francisco, by boat to San Diego, and finally by wagon to Aliso Canyon in a wandering search for land to homestead. They settled in a shack built and abandoned by Gene Salter. Today you can tour the old Thurston farm—it's now Ben Brown's Golf Course at The Ranch Laguna Beach (for more see Chapter 7).

The Thurstons survived by living off the land, hunting squirrels, rabbits and the occasional deer, gathering wild duck eggs from a nearby lagoon, and honey from wild bees. The father worked at the Irvine Ranch and took a milk cow in payment. They planted crops, then an orchard of walnut and olive trees, and bit-by-bit eked out a hardscrabble living. In later years they earned cash income selling produce to beach campers. Joseph S. Thurston, age three, lived the rest of his life in Laguna. Though he never attended school Joe wrote the best history of Laguna's founding in his memoir, *Laguna Beach of Early Days*. If you are visiting Laguna in hope of a day to remember, you might consider two from Joe Thurston's life, as described in his book:

Aliso Canyon and the old Thurston homestead. *Credit: First American, courtesy of the Laguna Beach Historical Society.*

The first came after the rest of his family grew up and moved away. Joe, now a young man, assumed responsibility for the farm—it was the only source of income for his mother Sarah now in Santa Ana and he felt a duty of care. Walking back to the family home one evening after a long day of farming he paused to look around the place where he had lived practically his whole life. Though everything was the same as before it was now different—he was the sole caretaker and everything depended on him. That evening, after a simple dinner, he was carried away by his thoughts, as recorded in his book:

> I simply got into a train of thought and travelled. I travelled into a land of harmony such as I had never known. This evening is one of two that stand out in my memory; the other was to come a few years later.

The other memorable evening of Joe's life involved . . . a woman. He had lived most of his life in solitude and was terribly deficient of social skills. He had admired a girl before, but was incapable of sharing his feelings. So the years passed in loneliness, farming, and traveling by wagon in the summer to sell his produce to the growing town. In town there were two small girls who greeted him with unusual friendliness. Their mother, Marie, was a schoolteacher and refugee from a marriage gone bad. Besides her daughters, Marie also cared for an invalid mother and a younger sister. Joe felt sympathy for Marie's heavy burden. And somehow, despite his poor sociability, that sympathy carried a message that Marie could appreciate.

Joe had bought land that ran along the hillside from Laguna Canyon to Bluebird Canyon. Wishing to help, he offered to build Marie a small home on a site she could select near her school. Marie selected a site she named "Dream Knoll." Here a cottage was constructed. So it happened that the second memorable evening of Joe Thurston's life came when Marie's home was nearly done. Inspecting the progress of construction with Marie, he was struck by the beauty of the world about him. Gazing out the back of the house, he saw a full moon rising over the eastern hills. Turning to the front door, he saw the sun setting over Catalina Island. And that is where Joe and Marie honeymooned after their marriage in the little community church down by Forest Avenue, on June 15, 1921.

Thurston Middle School, 2100 Park Avenue (originally Marie Thurston Junior High) remembers Marie's teaching service to the children of Laguna Beach. The two-room schoolhouse where she first taught still stands— moved down the hill to 384 Legion Street and renamed Veterans Memorial Building, but known as Legion Hall.

CHAPTER 29

The Rogers Group

The George and Lottie Rogers family homesteaded the downtown area, and built Laguna's first schoolhouse. *Photo: First American, courtesy of the Laguna Beach Historical Society.*

THE EARLY FAMILIES

In 1869 the transcontinental railroad was completed to Oakland, California and soon a railway was reaching down to southern California. That ribbon of steel gave the needed stimulus: In 1876 emigrants groups began to homestead government land around what would become Laguna Beach. The Thurston family (see Chapter 28), came from the Utah Territory in 1871, but the next emigrants came from Illinois and Minnesota in three extended family groups (known hereafter by the first name listed):

- The Rogers-Wayman-Prisk-Wilson-Edwards group
- The Hemenway-Brooks-Goff family
- The Thompson-French-Stevens-Loomis clan.

George and Lottie Rogers

The first settlers were busy homesteaders for within a few years the usable land was taken, excepting the land north of Broadway, part of the Irvine Ranch. George and Lottie Rogers purchased John Damron's 156-acres homestead for $1000 (including downtown Laguna between Broadway and Park Avenue). His father Henry homesteaded the hillside. George subdivided today's business district, naming Forest Avenue for the eucalyptus trees planted under the Timber Culture Act of 1873, which leads to a story of good intentions gone awry.

So many trees had been cut down to build the nation's railroads and fuel the locomotives that concerned citizens wondered when America's last tree would be taken. The intent of the Timber Culture law was to replace these and provide shade for our treeless prairies. Eucalyptus trees, imported from Australia, were widely planted and Laguna got several groves. Unfortunately, the wood was so tough and splintery it had little use though one good outcome was found: The *plein air* artists who came in the early 1900s, made beautiful paintings of the groves.

George and Lottie Rogers built a home—remembered as "the old ranch house"—where City Hall now stands along Forest Avenue. They also built Laguna's first school, little more than a shanty but a school nonetheless. Unfortunately George brought his lots to market just as the real estate boom was ending and unable to sell them, he returned to Missouri. His niece Ora Warling later visited him and purchased the ranch house plus downtown land.

Ora's husband Oscar used this land to partner with Nick Isch in the grandly named Isch & Warling Palace Stable. The Warlings later owned the Sandwich Mill restaurant, remembered for a group of writers and actors that met there for lunch and talk, including Erle Stanly Gardner and Boris Karloff.

CHAPTER 30
The Hemenway Clan

Harvey and Mariah Hemenway homesteaded in Laguna Canyon and named their farm Canyon Acres, remembered now by Canyon Acres Drive. The home they built, later reinforced with logs, became a favorite scene for artists. Two of his sisters also emigrated to Laguna. His sister Sylvia married Spencer Brooks and they had four children before his death—Nate, Will, Oliver, and Melissa—who all emigrated to Laguna with Sylvia. Melissa married William N Clapp, and Will married Anne Clapp so these early families were connected. Harvey's other sister, Elizabeth married Henry Goff, born in Connecticut. Henry homesteaded 51 acres below today's Park Avenue in downtown Laguna. He had three brothers—Leon (Lee), Franklin (Frank), and Hubbard (Hub)—and they homesteaded around Aliso Creek up to Arch Beach.

As noted in Chapter 29, George and Lottie Rogers purchased land between Laguna Creek (the southern edge of the Irvine Ranch) and Henry Goff's claim. Laguna Village, the older part of Laguna Beach, came from the Henry Goff and Rogers homesteads.

A Beach Resort

One reason for Laguna's charm is the town grew *organically*—meaning steady growth over a long time, unspoiled by any great plan, with nearly all the building done by local people, many of them artists, who planned to stay and live where they built. But the town had a close call with developers in the late 1880s. Frank and Lee Goff homesteaded coastal land north and south of Aliso Creek. Frank raised potatoes around today's Montage Laguna Beach resort and Treasure Island Park. The brothers also devised a method to harvest and sell the wild mustard seed, which grew freely in the hills.

At the peak of the 1880s real estate boom, investors came to town with the idea to build a railway depot and resort at Aliso Beach. They approached Lee Goff and he summoned enough chutzpah to ask $25,000—an unheard of price—for his coastal land. To his surprise the buyers agreed. Fearing that his brother Frank would ruin a good deal by asking too little, he sent a son secretly to wise him up. Frank got up enough courage to ask $14,000. The two Goff families took their winnings and moved away. The resort never happened due to the economic crash of the early 1890s. But over a century later one finally appeared—today's Montage Laguna Beach.

Henry Goff subdivided his Laguna beach property in 1883 and sold the first phase in two days. He later sold the balance of his holdings and returned to Missouri. There must be something to the term Connecticut Yankee because three of the Goff brothers—all Connecticut-born—made a killing in Laguna real estate and moved on. Only Hub, who mostly worked as a blacksmith, stayed to endure the tough times that followed and earn a place for himself as a Laguna founder. Joe Thurston, speaking of the Goff boys, remembered Hub as "the genius of the outfit," and it seems he was right.

7

Arch Beach

The three Brooks brothers mostly stayed around Laguna. **Will** wandered
some but finished his life here as the postman. **Nate** homesteaded
what became Arch Beach, discovered water in the hills above and
brought a pipeline down through Bluebird Canyon in the early 1880s.
This area developed first because of the scenic setting, available water,
and access by stagecoach through Aliso Canyon. Working with Hub
Goff (neighbor and brother-in-law to Nate's mom) they sold some land
for beach cottages. But Nate loved his land and kept most of it, even
through the hard times after the 1890 crash. Nate Brooks, more than
any other person, is considered the founder of Laguna Beach.

Oliver, who fought in the Civil War, was the eldest of the Brooks
brothers. He and wife Esther settled in Laguna where he was a partner in (and the captain of) the *Emma*, a converted whaling schooner
anchored near an Arch Beach pier built to Goff Island.

A Lesson Learned

Joe Thurston, in his book *Laguna Beach of Early Days*, remembers the
sudden end to the 1880s land boom:

> People began to come to California. Its fame had spread over
> the East, and the railroad companies had acquired a lot of land
> in the West. It was good business to encourage travel; also it
> made it possible to sell land. Stories went abroad telling how
> people had brought land and resold it making much money . . .
> [then] something happened. The banks stopped loaning money
> on real estate, and undertook to collect on what was already
> loaned. The next day there was about as much chance to sell
> land in California as there would be to reconstruct a bubble.

In the aftermath of the crash the little settlements, separated by
gulches at Sleepy Hollow, Bluebird Canyon, and Aliso Creek, sank into
a slumbering decline. The few hotels closed. Without the promise of
a profitable land sale, the harsh reality of farming on land without reli-
able water sank in. Many people moved away, sometimes taking their
homes with them by rolling them on logs.

A wise person might learn a lesson here. Those blessed with good
timing—think of the three Goff brothers—went away with a windfall.
Others, like George Rogers, missed the chance to cash in and left
penniless. But maybe the wisest were the ones like Nate Brookes,
Hub Goff, and Joe Thurston, who planted themselves in the ground,
accepted that they must work hard to earn a meager living, and found
enduring satisfaction in living by the beach.

Photo: David Laws

THE CHURCHES

Before there were churches in Laguna, people of faith gathered together for Sunday worship. Those groups grew into the congregations that formed the spiritual roots of Laguna Beach. Riverside Presbyterians funded our first town hall around 1900, for a place to meet. When outgrown they built a chapel, remembered as the Little Brown Church, near Forest Avenue on 2nd Street in 1915, and then the current sanctuary in 1928.

Early Catholics met at the old Mormon Schoolhouse, purchased after 1908 by Joseph and Catherine Yoch and donated for a church. In 1916 a Christian Science group began to meet in the Arch Beach Tavern, built a chapel at the corner of Glenneyre and Legion (now the Hare Krishna Temple), and later a larger building in Boat Canyon. The Reverend Percy Clarkson came to town in 1922 and formed two churches: St. Mary's Episcopal Church, and then St Francis-by-the-Sea, an American Catholic church. Clarkson was one of those colorful characters Laguna attracts.

8

In 1936 Mormon missionaries came to town and organized a Sunday school that met in various places, including the old Mormon Schoolhouse, now vacated by the Catholics, until their current chapel was built on Park Avenue. Finally the schoolhouse became the first home of Laguna's Little Church by the Sea. That old schoolhouse served Laguna in many ways and figured in the founding of three current churches. Church-going people still help to shape Laguna and this is part of what makes the town unique. If you find yourself in Laguna on a Sunday and really want to know the town, go to church! (See Chapter 32 for a list of churches.)

Laguna's early church history could be told by the travels of the old school-house (white building above with belfry). It started in Laguna Canyon in 1883 near El Toro Road, serving as both schoolhouse and chapel for a Missouri-based Mormon group. When those Mormons left in the crash of 1893, the schoolhouse was moved to near Canyon Acres Drive and used until a two-room schoolhouse opened in 1908. The Yoch family then bought the building and moved it into town (the location shown above), as the founding chapel for St. Joseph's Catholic Church. In 1931 noted artist Joseph Kleitsch bought it for a studio and moved it to the corner of Catalina and Legion but died shortly thereafter. Widow Kleitsch later leased it to a new Mormon congregation, and then to the Little Church by the Sea, who purchased it after her death and used it until a larger building was needed.

Other town buildings helped in the founding of Laguna's churches. The two-room schoolhouse that replaced the Mormon school became the Legion Hall when it was no longer needed and was used by the Mormons for a time, and then by the Christian Science church. Those old buildings played a role in the founding of Laguna, as well as the churches that shaped our town. *Photo: First American, Courtesy of Laguna Beach Historical Society*

CHAPTER 31

The First Churches

Spiritual Roots

In our quest to explain the origins of Laguna's uniqueness, we now come to the churches. In early Laguna most people were part of one church or another. In the 1920 U.S. Census, for example, just 361 people are listed. That's the population. Yet there are three churches: the Presbyterians in the "little brown chapel" on 2nd Street, the Catholics at the old Mormon Schoolhouse, and a Christian Science group using a room of the Arch Beach Tavern. On Sundays I suppose there was seating for over half the town. So in the beginning, churches were an important influence.

Today, there are 14 chapels in use plus several groups worshipping wherever they can. Though church attendance is a lower percentage than before, it's still significant. And in the way that the pendulum of society swings back and forth, I expect more will become churchgoers in some future day. In this chapter we remember the founding of the early (pre-WWII) churches.

Mormons

In the 1870s just about all the homesteading families included some kind of Mormon. These weren't the type settling the Utah Territory, shocking the country with the practice of polygamy, though a few had come from there. Joe Thurston tells of this in his memoir, *Laguna Beach of Early Days*. In that time, the scattered families would gather together on Saturday night to socialize and dance to Hub Goff's fiddle. The Thurstons had come from Utah and Joe, a boy at the time, remembers:

> There were quite a number of people who had settled in Laguna Canyon and at the beach . . . many of these people also belonged to the [Mormon] church [but] did not dance. While the Mormons of Utah encouraged dancing, and these people claimed to be Mormons, they considered it a sin to dance, so if any of them came the evening would be spent playing games . . . [like] "post office.". . . Just why it was a sin to dance and not a sin to play kissing games, we never did find out.

The first church in Laguna belonged to a Missouri-based splinter group of the Mormon Church. Founded in 1879, it disbanded in 1893 after key families moved away following the real estate crash. In 1936 two

8

young missionaries of the Mormon Church headquartered in Utah came to Laguna Beach and organized members scattered along the coast into a Sunday school. The church grew steadily over the years and built its current meeting hall across from the high school in 1951. At that time the area of the church covered the Saddleback Valley from the Irvine Ranch down to Oceanside. Now fifty or so congregations have formed in the original area and the Laguna chapel is reduced almost to the city limits.

A "woodie" in front of the Laguna Presbyterian Church.
Photo: April Hellewell Dickson

Laguna Presbyterian Church

When Henry Goff first offered $50 beachfront lots in 1883, prosperous Riverside families were the first buyers. The Riverside wealth came from "orange gold," or citrus farming. "Captain" Benjamin Handy, a horticulturist, built the second home on the bluff and on summer Sundays became the acting minister.

Sylvanus and Sabra Ferris, successful citrus growers who had helped build Riverside's Magnolia Avenue Presbyterian Church, also built a cottage. Mrs. Ferris, to use a term of the time, was a progressive woman; besides her own family she reared two orphaned children, and supported the WCTU, the group most responsible for Prohibition. So when the Ferris family came to Laguna, they "brought their religion with them."

Seeking a place for Sunday meetings, the Riverside people donated $100 to build a town hall (a significant sum at that time, considering the price of their lots). The town got behind the project and the building, known as the "Pavilion," became a place for Sunday School, as well as socials, dances, town meetings, weddings, and funerals. Sunday School attendance increased and by 1914 the Pavilion was too small. The Ferris family donated two lots on 2nd Street and with the help of a visiting minister a community church remembered as the "little brown chapel" was built. In 1917 it was organized as the Community Presbyterian Church with 17 founding members. The Rev. Raymond I. Brahams became pastor in 1925; in his 24 years of service the present building on Forest Avenue was dedicated and became the main church of Laguna Beach. (The stained glass window overlooking 2nd Street is a memorial gift by the Ferris children.) A social hall and school followed—Rev. Brahams is remembered as "a builder of character and churches." The building was recently renovated to meet earthquake standards under the guidance of Rev. Arthur Jerry Tankersley, pastor since 1972.

St. Catherine Catholic Church

Joseph and Catherine (Kate) Yoch of Santa Ana were devout Catholics. Joseph invested in Laguna land and owned the old Laguna Beach Hotel. Kate's brother Nick Isch operated the grocery store-post office and co-owned the Isch Warling Palace Stable. He and wife Katherine (Kit) were also Catholics. To help start a church, Yoch purchased the old Mormon Schoolhouse in 1908 after it was replaced by a new building, moved it to land he owned on today's Catalina Street (see photo on page 100), and this became St. Joseph's, then at his wish to honor his wife, St. Catherine of Sienna Catholic Church. The church grew with the city and later moved to the present facility at 1042 Temple Terrace, followed by a parish school at 30516 S. Coast Highway.

First Church of Christ Scientist

The Christian Science church, with its focus on faith healing and the reading of scripture, was an influence in early Laguna. Meetings started by 1916, first in the home of Mary E. Watrous, then in a room of the Arch Beach Tavern. Founders include the Peacock, Skidmore, Overton, and Wilson families, familiar names in Laguna history. A chapel was built at Legion and Glenneyre in 1937 (now the Hare Krishna Temple) and a reading room, a place for the public to read and meditate, opened at 284 Forest Avenue in 1947. The church expanded to their 635 High Drive building in 1968.

St. Mary's Episcopal Church

This church has graced Park Avenue since 1925, though in the beginning it had another name. There's a story behind the name change, documented by Starr Ramsey Helms in her 2012 book, *The Lost Chapel of St Francis Hill*. Percy Clarkson (1875-1942), remembered as a "colorful and popular" figure, had founded one church in Orange and was sent to Laguna in 1922 to found a "summer chapel." He did more, purchasing six lots, and convincing his Episcopal leaders to sign a mortgage. By 1925 Clarkson had constructed a church he named St. Francis-by-the-Sea.

In time doctrinal differences emerged between Clarkson and his superiors and his resignation was forced when he filed to divorce his wife in 1927. The divorce petition was cancelled but Clarkson left to found his own church, taking half the parish and the church name. What remained became St. Mary's Episcopal Church but it was a church without a building because though the Episcopal Church held the mortgage on the property, the title was held in Clarkson's name. Eventually the church retired the mortgage and reached a compromise wherein Clarkson surrendered the three lots on which the church stood, but kept the other lots, which included the parsonage. Clarkson then became a priest for a branch of the American Catholic Church, built a tiny cathedral that he named St. Francis-by-the-Sea, and in effect invented his own privately owned church where he was free to preach as he wished. So there they sit today, side by side, two churches founded by one man, each serving its parishioners, though differently.

To fully appreciate Laguna Beach, try attending one of the churches during your visit. I don't think you'll regret it. For details, see Chapter 32.

On Any Given Sunday

The chapel for the LDS (Mormon) Church, across from the high school on Park Avenue, was dedicated in 1951. Congregation boundaries covered most of the Saddleback Valley in the beginning, but just Laguna Beach today. *Photo: April Hellewell Dickson*

On any given Sunday, in addition to discovering Laguna's spiritual roots, you just might hear a needed message. You can also meet some great people at the church of your choice. That's all I'm going to say, except you'll likely be the better for going. The churches:

Chabad Jewish Center (30804 S. Coast Hwy; 949/499 0770) holds services Friday at 7:00 p.m. and Saturday 10:30 a.m.

Christian Science Church (635 High Drive, 949/494 3040; also has a Reading Room, 284 Forest Ave, phone 949/494 4503, open during the week). Sunday worship at 635 High Drive, 10:00 a.m. Read the history in Chapter 31.

Hare Krishna Temple (285 Legion St., 949/494 7029) has Sunday service from 5:00 p.m. to 8:00 p.m., ending with dinner. In the '70s the devotees, remembered for saffron gowns and shaven heads, were chanting in the streets. It's quieter now, but you can still count on an interesting experience.

Jehovah's Witnesses (20912 Castle Rock Road, out in Laguna Canyon, 949/494 5815) has 1:30 p.m. Sunday meeting.

8

Laguna Presbyterian Church (415 Forest Ave, 949/494 7555) offers Sunday worship at 8:30 a.m. and 10:00.   A venerable building due to its history on Forest Avenue (see Chapter 31).

Laguna Beach United Methodist Church (21632 Wesley Drive in south Laguna, 949/499 3088) holds Sunday services at 10:00 a.m.

Little Church by the Sea (468 Legion St., 949/494 6191) offers services at 9:00 and 10:30 a.m. Laguna's version of the old time religion; dress is casual.

Mormon Church (The Church of Jesus Christ of Latter-day Saints, 682 Park Avenue, across from the high school) services begin at 10:00 a.m. Sunday morning.

Neighborhood Congregational Church (340 St. Ann's Drive, 949/494 8061), Sunday services at 10:00 a.m.

St. Catherine of Siena Catholic Church (1042 Temple Terrace, 949/494 9701) offers Sunday Mass at 7:30 a.m., 9:00, 11:00, 1:30 (Spanish), and 5:30. See history in Chapter 31.

St. Francis by-the-Sea Cathedral (430 Park Avenue) offers American Catholic mass 9:30 a.m. Sundays in this jewel box cathedral.

St. Mary's Episcopal Church (428 Park Avenue, 949/494 3542) services start at 8:00 a.m. and 10:30 a.m. Read about this building in Chapter 31.

South Shores Church (37212 Crown Valley Parkway, Dana Point, 949/496 9331) isn't technically in Laguna Beach but did get its start in a Laguna gallery back in the '50s. Baptist services in the traditional style at 8:15 and 9:30 a.m.; contemporary at 11:00 a.m.

Unitarian Universalist Church (429 Cypress Drive, 949/497 4568) holds Sunday services at 10:00 a.m. Chartered in 1948, it's California's 2nd oldest congregation.

THE LAGUNA GREENBELT

I don't know if there's anything quite like the Laguna Greenbelt—over 22,000 acres of land developers would die for, purchased by the people with the simple goal of giving it back to Nature.

The land came from two early ranches: the Irvine Ranch to the north, and the Moulton Niguel Ranch to the east. James Irvine's land was the former *Rancho San Joaquin*, granted to Jose Sepulveda in 1842. Lewis F. Moulton, with the help of Basque partner Jean Pierre Daguerre, built the Moulton Niguel Ranch from Juan Avila's *Rancho Niguel* and the western part of Jose Serrano's *Rancho Canada de los Alisos*. The contributions of these families to Laguna include the *Irvine Bowl*, site of the Pageant of the Masters, and the Laguna Playhouse's *Moulton Theatre*.

The Laguna Greenbelt wouldn't have happened without a local bookseller turned visionary named James (Jim) Dilley, the subject of Chapter 33.

A spring view of Woods Canyon wrapped in morning mist. *Photo: David Laws*

9

Jim Dilley's Dream

Bonnie, here with Jim, presided over Dilley's Books. *Photo: Courtesy of the Laguna Beach Independent.*

Jim Dilley had passed but Jeanette Dilley, his former wife, was our neighbor when we moved to Laguna Beach. Mrs. Dilley lived in a modest bungalow across the street and we understood she was the widow of the man behind the Laguna Greenbelt. We called her Mrs. Dilley because "Jeanette" seemed too informal for this intelligent lady.

Jim and Jeanette were married at Menlo Park in 1957 and a year later they opened a bookstore in Laguna Beach—Dilley's Books. They started on Forest Avenue but Mrs. Dilley jumped at the chance to buy the 540 S. Coast building, their location until Dilley's closed in 1982, after Jim's death from cancer. Jim studied for a PhD at Harvard Divinity School, though he was never a minister, and Mrs. Dilley's graduate work included an MS in statistics. Their education predicted their roles in the business: he was an amiable pipe-smoking presence, filled with love for his books, a bit reluctant to see them leave. She was the watchful overseer who kept a close eye on the daily receipts. Together they created a business remembered with much fondness.

The third party to the success of Dilley's Books was their collie Bonnie, who greeted visitors. Jim loved his dog, as did Jeanette, but Bonnie grew old and Jim finally took her to the vet who recommended, out of compassion, she be put to sleep. When Jim reported back to Jeanette that he had done this (without her consent), she was very upset. Upset enough to ask for a divorce. Poor Jim—he lost not only his beloved dog, but also his wife and business partner. A divorce is rarely about one thing, you know, and it's true that Jim was a man who heard distant drums. But he was incomplete without Jeanette, had no mind for the details of running the store, and the business began to fail.

Fong Imports was next door to Dilley's, specializing in Asian jewelry. Mrs. Fong, both neighbor and friend, was pained by the decline of Dilley's Books. To her eye, Jim was ruining the business while Jeanette sat home. So she arranged a reconciliation that brought Jeanette back into the store. Things got better; Jeanette restored order and Jim found a new collie to greet customers. The Dilleys, for she had kept his surname, were still a good team and most were unaware of the divorce.

It's not good to speak ill of the deceased. But it's a fact that Jim once had a drinking problem. The Laguna police had picked Jim up enough times that his dog Bonnie would jump into any police car with an open door. So Jim joined Alcoholics Anonymous and became sober in 1963, which led to two other outcomes. First, when he died in 1980 Jim left his bookstore building to the Laguna AA group to fund a meeting place. The result, known as The Canyon Club by its location at 20456 Laguna Canyon Road, is an enduring benefit of Dilley's recovery.

The other benefit is the main point of this story. Jim enjoyed traveling and in England was taken with the garden city movement, an early vision of city planning which surrounded smaller cities with "greenbelts." (The early Laguna architect Jean Louis Egasse had apprenticed in the garden city of Letchworth, outside of London.) The idea of people living close to such parklands had great appeal to him. Consequently, in the '60s when planned communities were sprouting like weeds around Orange County, a different vision grew in Jim Dilley's head.

In 1968 Jim Dilley revealed his impossible dream—Laguna Beach surrounded by land purchased with public funds and given back to Nature, never to be "developed." This was also the year Laguna restored Main Beach as a "window to the sea" (see Chapter 2). So there was a precedent, but Jim's vision was far more ambitious. Main

Beach was a few acres; Jim was thinking thousands of acres. In an *L. A. Times* interview he admitted to being, "quixotic, carried away with the cause."

The remarkable thing is that Jim Dilley's impossible dream came to pass. He did it by forming a grassroots organization under the non-profit conservation organization Laguna Greenbelt, Inc. and then convincing people, one-by-one, neighborhood by neighborhood, to share his vision. As a result the city bought Sycamore Hills in 1978, the parcel Jim called, "the buckle of the greenbelt." That land—roughly the triangle between El Toro Road and Laguna Canyon Road that includes Barbara Lake, Orange County's only natural lake—is now the James Dilley Greenbelt Preserve.

After Jim's death in 1980 his Greenbelt group marched on. The turning point was a $20 million Laguna bond election in 1990 to purchase 2000 acres in Laguna and Laurel Canyons for open space. The land had been approved for a 2500-home development but the bond passed with an 80% super majority energized by two events: First, Laguna artists, underwritten by the Festival of Arts, created "The Tell," a 630-foot photo-mural erected along Laguna Canyon Road. The Tell spoke against development of the costal canyons. The second event was a massive public march up Laguna Canyon Road by 7500 concerned citizens. Jim had been gone for nine years at the time of the march, but on that day his unlikely vision was very much alive. The Laguna Coast Wilderness Park officially opened in 1993. The combined parks around Laguna now comprise an "urban wilderness" exceeding 22,000 acres.

The *L. A. Times* once described Jim Dilley as "the improbable leader of the impossible dream." Jim was guilty on both counts. But his vision rang true with the public and their grassroots efforts made it real, leaving a lasting treasure for Laguna Beach. Which begs this question: Has any person done more for our city than that "improbable leader" Jim Dilley? I think not, and surely this was the other benefit of his hard won sobriety.

(Sources include Elizabeth Brown, president of Laguna Greenbelt Inc. and Carol Croissant, executrix for Mrs. Jeanette Dilley.)

CHAPTER 34

Enjoying Laguna's Wilderness

The Laurel Canyon hiking trail, with creek in late autumn flow. *Photo: Ronald H. Chilcote, "Nature's Laguna Wilderness," Laguna Wilderness Press, 2003.*

Take a hike! Our Laguna Greenbelt, the original name for the 22,000-acre nature preserve envisioned by Jim Dilley, includes four parklands (from north to south): Crystal Cove State Park (with El Moro Canyon), Laguna Coast wilderness Park, City of Irvine Open Space Preserve, and Aliso & Woods Canyon Wilderness Park. These areas, excepting roadways and access facilities, exist as they have for millennia. For the complete Laguna experience, explore these wilderness areas by hiking, biking, or horseback. For the latter two you'll need a bike or horse; there are also guided walks. For detailed information visit http://ocparks.com/parks/lagunac/.

To enjoy the wilderness areas closest to Laguna Beach, here are various access points to the trails of the parks that also include parking and basic facilities:

9

• **Crystal Cove State Park:** Besides the beach, there are seventeen miles of hiking trails (parking $18/day) at 8471 N. Pacific Coast Highway. (Directions: From Main Beach, drive 2.4 miles north on Coast Highway to park entrance.)

• **Laguna Coast Wilderness Park:** Has 40 miles of hiking trails emanating from three trailheads along Laguna Canyon Road ($3/day parking). The trailheads (with distance from Main Beach):

-**Big Bend** (2.2 miles from Main Beach) offers equestrian trails (and parking for your horse trailer) as well as bike trails.

-**Willow Canyon** (3.1 miles) has a small nature center plus trails to Willow and Laurel Canyons, and beyond. It's a good place for your first hike.

-**Nix Nature Center** (5 miles) is the headquarters, with trails to Little Sycamore Canyon, Barbara's Lake in the James Dilley Preserve, etc.

• **Aliso and Woods Canyons Wilderness Park:** The 30 miles of trails in this Orange County park can be accessed from Laguna Niguel (parking lot at 28373 Alicia Parkway), or from two unattended Laguna Beach Parks:

-**Alta Laguna Park** is reached by taking Park Avenue up to Top of the World neighborhood then turning left on Alta Laguna; the park will be on the right.

-**Moulton Meadows Park** is accessed by driving up Nyes Place to Arch Beach Heights, then turning left on Balboa road. The park will be on the right.

A HIKE IN LAUREL CANYON

DIRECTIONS: From Main Beach, take Laguna Canyon Road 3.1 miles to the Willow Canyon parking area and trailhead. Buy a $3 parking permit and stop by the nature center for a trail map.

The best way to appreciate the wilderness areas surrounding Laguna Beach is to take a hike. The Laurel Canyon trail is a good place to start; it includes a grassy meadow, a winding trail that follows a dry creek upward as the canyon narrows, and broad vistas from the saddle at the top. The climb isn't hard but enough to make it a workout.

A Laguna Canyon wilderness panorama: Coastal sagebrush, a grove of sycamore trees, and distant hills invite the hiker. *Photo: Ronald H. Chilcote, "Nature's Laguna Wilderness," Laguna Wilderness Press, 2003.*

On our first hike we took the Laurel Canyon Spur trail to Willow Canyon and returned via the Willow Canyon Trail. Along the way there are posts marking stations with telephone numbers to get recorded information about sights along the trail. Our small group included three generations, ranging in age from 4 (a good hiker considering his age) to 72, and everyone found interesting sights along the trail. We paused for a snack at the top and completed the trip in about two hours. On the trail we saw family groups, couples, and individuals, some hiking, others mountain biking, all friendly folks enjoying a day of nature. You can't really know Laguna until you're hiked its wilderness trails.

I hope this meandering tour has made you a believer that there's no place quite like Laguna.

As we've said, the roots of Laguna's uniqueness began with those early homesteaders. The artists documented the primal beauty of Laguna's coves and created our cultural foundations—the Museum, Festival, and Pageant. Early architects created our charming cottages and castles. Merchants built hotels, restaurants, galleries, and all the rest. Watermen (and women) showed us the joy of wave riding, whether as surfers or skimboarders. One man—Eiler Larsen, the Laguna Greeter— taught the importance of unfeigned friendliness. And ardent conservations convinced us of the importance of preserving Nature—the small town of Laguna is graced by the country's second largest urban wilderness, our Greenbelt.

It bears repeating: There's no place quite like Laguna. When some unusual thing occurs here, you're likely to hear the phrase, said with a roll of the eyes, "Only in Laguna." Whether you're resident or visitor,

Laguna is a place to step out of the daily hustle and bustle, dig your feet into the sand, and savor life. And that's the goal of this book—to live as fully as one can, by loving Laguna.

Looking back, it was an audacious mission to explain Laguna's uniqueness plus give a guide to the town in 116 pages. It demanded Hemingwayesque brevity—so many stories deserve a fuller telling. But we held to our goal of a book you could fit in your jacket pocket but also want on your bookshelf. Do you remember the fable of the six blind men from Indostan who encountered the elephant? How each imagined it differently according to what part he touched, whether leg, tusk, trunk or ear? Laguna is like that. This guide is based on the parts that we have touched in our years here, and what has touched us. Others may experience Laguna differently. If you want to share your experience or have an idea for future editions, please write to: skip@lovinglaguna.com. Thanks for reading.

A time exposure of Crescent Bay as the sunrise reveals another perfect day. Photo: David Laws

INDEX